Exploring the Spiritual Dimension in Caring

Edited by
E S Farmer

Quay
Books

Quay Books

Mark Allen Publishing Limited, Jesses Farm, Snow Hill, Dinton
Salisbury, Wiltshire, SP3 5HN WY24
ETmics / Religion

British Library Cataloguing-in-Publication Data
A catalogue record is available for this book

© Mark Allen Publishing Limited, 1996

ISBN 1 85642 119 8

Printed in the UK by Biddles Limited, Guildford

Exploring the Spiritual Dimension in Caring

Contents

List of contributors

Ann Bradshaw, Macmillan Clinical Fellow at the National Institute for Nursing, Oxford, trained as an SRN from 1968–1971 at the Radcliffe Infirmary, Oxford. She worked as a Staff Nurse and District Nurse in several different hospitals and specialities including St Joseph's Hospice in Hackney before leaving nursing to bring up a family. In order to reorientate herself with the changes on her return to nursing, she studied for the Diploma in Nursing at Bristol Polytechnic from 1986–1989. Surprised and perplexed by the new theories and values now being taught and wanting to think more deeply about them, she began working for a MPhil which turned into a PhD thesis entitled 'Towards a definition of the spiritual dimension and its implications for nursing practice and patient care.' This was successfully completed in 1992 and a revised version has been published by Scutari Press in 1994 entitled 'Lighting the Lamp: the spiritual dimension of nursing'. Ann is currently working on a book charting the changes which have reconstructed nursing's ethical tradition and looking at their implications for patient care. She is also working as a practical clinical staff nurse in both the care of the elderly and a hospice.

Brian Devlin was born in 1960 and was brought up in Fife in Scotland. In 1978, he entered the Roman Catholic Seminary to train for RC Priesthood and was ordained Priest for the Archdiocese of St Andrews and Edinburgh after completing his studies.

Following continuing theological unease with the Roman Catholic Church's teaching on various ethical matters, Brian resigned from the Priesthood in 1986. As the HIV/AIDS outbreak hit the drug-using community in Edinburgh, Brian worked as a Project Officer for a drop-in drug counselling centre for, mainly heroin addicts. He then became National Training and Counselling Officer for Scottish AIDS Monitor and was also responsible for the development of the Buddy support system in Scotland. This scheme was also used in a pilot project for some of Scotland's main prisons. In 1989, Brian noved north to Inverness to take up the post of Highland AIDS Liaison Officer which was jointly funded by the Highland Regional Council, the Highland Health Board and the District Councils. After four years, Brian was promoted to the post of Harm Reduction Manager within the Health Promotion Department of the Highland Health Board and was responsible for all the health promotion programmes of the area department. These included programmes on alcohol, drug taking, AIDS, coronary heart disease, and nutrition. He now holds the position of Public/Information Officer and is responsible for the external and internal communication strategies of the Board on a local and national level.

Betty Farmer RGN, SCM, DN, PhD is a Reader in Nursing at Highland & W Isles College of Nursing in association with the University of Abertay Dundee. Betty has wide experience in general nursing, management and research and is the Director of the Scottish Highlands Centre for Human Caring in Inverness, Scotland, which is first international affiliate of the Center for Human Caring, University of Colorado

David Lunan was born 1944. He is Minister at Renfield St Stephen's in Glasgow, is married with four sons. He is former Convener of the Church of Scotland's Committee of Health and Healing.

Jean Watson RN, PhD, FAAN is Distinguished Professor of Nursing and previously Dean of the School of Nursing, Health

Sciences Center, University of Colorado. Jean is one of nursing's most eminent nurse theorists and is internationally renowned for her work on caring and healing. In 1986, Jean established the Center for Human Caring at the University of Colorado, is Director of the Center and current President of the National League for Nursing, USA.

Prologue

Dr E S Farmer

'We are living in the midst of a scientific revolution whose philosophical and spiritual meaning is far from clear to most of us.'

Renee Weber

In July 1993, the Scottish Highlands Centre for Human Caring sponsored a conference with the somewhat unusual title: 'Exploring the Spirituality of Caring'. The impetus for this event is to some extent expressed in the above quotation from a book on holistic nursing practice (Dossey *et al*, 1988). Holism is a concept that views everything in terms of patterns of organisations, relationships, interactions and processes that combine to form a whole. The increasing emphasis on holism in nursing is a consequence of stunning and controversial new ideas in physics and astronomy which are only now being addressed by the wider community of scholars — including nurses.

Over the past 50 years, four momentous theories have been postulated: the theory of relativity, quantum mechanics, chaos theory and holographic theory (Davies, 1983; Gleick, 1988; Bohm and Peat, 1989; Atkins, 1992). The new paradigm science of interconnectedness derived from these theories is incompatible with the Renaissance paradigm formalised by Descartes and Newton which proposed that nature could be reduced to a series of building blocks and forces and mechanisms through which these interact, ultimately leading to absolute control and prediction (Pelletier, 1985; Capra, *et al*, 1992). In the new paradigm, the relationship between the parts and the whole is reversed. Ultimately, there are no parts at all. It is postulated that what was previously called a part is merely a pattern in an intrinsically dynamic, inseparable web of relationships (Davies, 1983; Capra *et al*, 1992). Where it was believed that scientific knowledge could achieve absolute certainty, it is now recognised that all concepts and theories are limited and approximate. The new paradigm is of considerable importance to the health sciences. The reductionist, mechanistic science of Descartes and Newton separates body, mind and soul; the new scientific paradigm makes no such distinction. The cure–care dichotomy, which emanates from the view of people as being no more than the sum of their parts, cannot prevail in systems and process-oriented science.

The new ideas about time, space and consciousness have turned science on its head and demand a radical reconstruction of the most fundamental aspects of contemporary life. It is argued that science is beginning to answer deep questions of existence — how did the universe begin and how will it end? What is matter? What is life? What is mind? (Pelletier, 1985; Bohm and Peat, 1989; Capra *et al*, 1992.) Science and religion have been the major driving forces in the history of mankind. These systems of thought have long been seen as incompatible and antagonistic, and both have been sources of conflict, suffering and destruction throughout history (Capra, 1983; Davies, 1983; Atkins, 1992). Religion is founded on dogma, unalterable truths, whereas science makes scepticism a virtue and readily accommodates change. Propositions about the impact of the new integrative science on religion range from rejection of the need for a creator (Atkins 1992) to a belief in an impending unification of science and religion (Scott Peck, 1978; Davies, 1983; Wilkie Au, 1990; Capra *et al*, 1992).

It is argued that theology needs to revise its map of reality. In its proper sense 'dogma' is a statement about reality (an opinion). As such, it is an approximation not an absolute. The sum of religious dogmas cannot, therefore, be revealed truth (Capra *et al*, 1992). Science now accepts mystery, the mystical, and suggests that a more adequate concept of the deity is the unfolding of God's Kingdom as historical reality, worked out by humans in the process of living in time. In that sense, God is immanent, and spiritual growth is the evolution of an individual through dialogue with the spirit which is the unconscious self. Spiritual growth occurs when there is synchrony of the conscious and unconscious mind. The key that opens the door to the unconscious is volitional love.

Clearly, these radical ideas have provoked heated debate and, no doubt, will result in hostility, violence and repression which are, regrettably, characteristics of scientific revolutions. Nevertheless, it is a debate which nurses must enter into. The consequences of failure to address such fundamental issues are too grave to contemplate.

The papers given at the conference and included in this volume are offered as a contribution to the debate that must take place in nursing and in the wider context of health care provision. Ann Bradshaw's chapter puts the debate in context. She argues that nursing is fundamentally a loving response to the human being created in the image of God. Focusing on the inconsistencies of nursing philosophies, she argues that nursing should return to its covenantal foundation and pastoral model of care. Jean Watson holds that caring is the 'heart and substance of nursing' and also calls for nurses to acknowledge the spiritual — to connect it with the Infinite and Divine through our 'heart-felt practices'. From his pastoral work as a Church of Scotland minister, David Lunan provides illustrations of healing through the power of love and prayer, and, from an ethical perspective, Brian Devlin offers his thoughts on progression towards a fuller humanity.

In July 1985, Jean Watson, Ann Bradshaw and David Lunan were brought together again to continue the debate at an intensive workshop for 53 American nursing students which was sponsored by the Helene Fuld Health Trust and hosted by the Scottish Highlands Centre for Human Caring. The most striking development in the two years between the first and second events was that the views expressed by Jean Watson and Ann Bradshaw seemed to be less polarised. The speakers were not invited to prepare papers for publication in advance of the workshop since it was not intended that there should be a formal product of the event. However, Ann Bradshaw had in fact prepared a paper which it was felt should complete this volume because it succinctly presents the issues and clears the way for what is hoped will be a continuing scholarly debate on the spiritual dimension in caring.

References

Atkins P (1992) *Creation Revisited. The Origin of Space, Time and the Universe.* Penguin Books, London

Bohm D, Peat FD (1989) *Science, Order and Creativity.* Routledge, London

Capra F (1983) *The Turning Point. Science, Society and the Rising Culture.* Flamingo, London

Capra F, Steindl-Rast D, Matus T (1992) *Belonging to the Universe. New Thinking About God and Nature.* Penguin Books, London

Davies P (1983) *God and the New Physics.* Penguin Books, London

Dossey BM, Keegan L, Guzetta CE, Kolkmeier LG (1988) *Holistic Nursing. A Handbook for Practice.* Aspen Publishers Inc, Maryland

Gleick J (1988) *Chaos.* Cardinal, London

Pelletier KR (1985) *Toward a Science of Consciousness.* Berkeley, California

Scott Peck M (1978) *The Road Less Travelled.* Simon and Schuster, New York

Wilkie Au SJ (1990) *By Way of the Heart. Toward a Holistic Christian Spirituality.* Geoffrey Chapman, London

Chapter 1

Lighting the lamp: The covenant as an encompassing framework for the spiritual dimension of nursing care*

Ann Bradshaw

What is the spiritual dimension of caring? The unnamed writer of the chapter 'Spiritual and religious aspects of care' in *Mud and Stars* (Working Party, 1991: 152), a book about hospice care, asserts that religion and the spiritual can and should be separated. The writer states that:

> *'While everyone has a spiritual dimension, in Britain today only a minority practise a formal religion. Hence, although people commonly say "I am not religious", they do not say "I am not spiritual".'*

---

*   Lecture given in July 1993, Inverness.

In the author's view, the spiritual dimension transcends and holds together the physical, psychological and social dimensions:

'...[it] integrates the other three dimensions into an "I", an individual who is more than the sum of his parts.'

What are the grounds for this assertive statement? On the one hand, theologians would disagree. The spiritual dimension is not merely the isolated 'I' of the individual, but the 'I' in relation to God. On the other hand, if, as the *Mud and Stars'* writer states, the spiritual dimension is the essential 'I', then as psychologists argue, it is purely human psychology and indeed, for behaviourists, the effects of chemicals in the brain.

If there is doubt in determining the spiritual nature of the person, there will inevitably be difficulty in knowing what, if any, is the spiritual dimension of care. This is now a vigorous debate in nursing and this chapter seeks to examine both contemporary modernist and traditional theological approaches to this issue from the perspective of nursing theory.

Setting the context for the debate

During the 1970s, there was a sea-change in British nursing as it turned to North American nursing for its models of care. This seems to have been partly as a reaction to nursing's handmaiden image as a servant to medicine and so an attempt to professionalise British nursing by defining a distinctive body of nursing knowledge to give nursing academic status. It was also, as will be explored later, a probably unintentional result of allowing theological principles to become eroded and attenuated and so marginal in care.

Nevertheless, the explicit sea-change in the theoretical underpinnings of British nursing involved, however unintentionally at first, a rejection of nursing tradition and therein a total reinterpretation of nursing history through the secular revisionist eyes of Marxist and feminist writers. The long-held, Judaeo-Christian, ethical tradition of caring for the sick as an altruistic spiritual calling was now seen as archaic, irrelevant and even a dangerous myth that needed dispelling — the opiate of oppressed nurses.

This forceful rejection of nursing as essentially a spiritual vocation resting in the biblical principle of the light of God, and evoked by the image of Nightingale with her lamp at Scutari, draws a vivid analogy with Nietzsche's (1974) parable of the madman. The madman takes a lighted lamp in the day-time to the market place to search for God, but discovering God is dead he finally smashes the lamp in disgust.

In Nietzsche's view it is only a madman who looks for God. The values of the lamp tradition are now cast aside as the lamp lies broken. This breaking of the nursing lamp, the fracturing of the theological basis for the original spiritual framework of care, as this chapter seeks to argue and demonstrate, has resulted in the fragmentation of care, a splitting apart of the personal and relational from the technical and functional, and with it the loss of the moral foundation for nursing care itself.

Yet all nursing theorists are themselves dependent on their undergirding philosophy. The nature of the human being upon which they build their models of care determines how the spiritual dimension of such care, and its implications for both the patient and the nurse, is interpreted and incorporated into practice.

North American nursing, influenced educationally by Dewey's philosophical pragmatism and hence his optimistic belief in scientific progress, may have been quicker to reject traditional theological principles than its British counterpart. Annie Goodrich (1932), the North American nursing professor writing in the early decades of the twentieth century, seems to espouse a similar atheistic liberal humanism to Dewey, whom she quotes. Like him, she rejects the concept of the metaphysical in favour of ultimate human concerns grounded in aesthetic, scientific or moral experience.

Despite philosophical incoherence in many North American nursing theories, the influence of pragmatism is clearly apparent. Just as philosophical pragmatism is inherently unstable bending with Dewey towards objectivity and empiricism, or with James into subjectivity and existentialism (James, 1960; Thayer, 1964;

Macquarrie, 1972; Ayer, 1978), so nursing theorists reflect this uncertainty in their own theories of care.

Interpretations of the spiritual dimension of care are therefore either external descriptions of the sense data of human activity or the phenomenological disclosure of the inner-lived experience of human existence. It is this existential phenomenological strand of theory that has given rise to transcendental theories of caring.

The sociocultural approach to the spiritual dimension of care

The philosophical basis

Nursing theories that take predominantly materialistic approaches to the human being and focus particularly on the body as a set of mechanistic systems, tend to a utilitarian conception of the spiritual dimension of care. In Kantian fashion the phenomenon of existence, the manner in which people exhibit their belief systems through organised religion, is separated from the unknowable essence of life which underpins beliefs and values. This sociocultural approach to religion relies on a value-free scientific basis which does not differentiate between religious doctrines and values because it is not concerned with what Kant (1977) called the noumenon — any metaphysical, unknowable truth.

This strand of nursing theory follows the sociological positions of Durkheim (1915) and Weber (1965) by focusing on external religious practices on the one hand, and the moral, ethical self on the other. Although the methods of Durkheim and Weber differ, both focus on structure, the external phenomenon, rather than truth, the unknowable noumenon. Similarly, this strand of nursing follows the approach of cognitive and developmental psychologists such as Piaget and Kohlberg (Fowler, 1981), who view religion not from the issue of truth but as a validator for moral values, the Kantian categorical imperative of practical reason.

Sociocultural nursing approaches

Virginia Henderson (1969) sees nursing as predominantly the regulation of physiological systems, and her approach exemplifies the sociocultural view of the spiritual nature of nursing care. She distinguishes between, on the one hand, culturally determined religious beliefs and practices, and on the other, the ethical, moral and spiritual dimension of the self which validates personal behaviour. Under the heading 'Helping patient practice his religion or conform to his concept of right and wrong', Henderson identifies religious practices as the functional activities that satisfy human longing for faith, and describes the nurse's role as to be informed about such practices in order to support them for her patients.

However, she is explicit in her position that it is not possible to identify any truth in such longings or to differentiate between differing cultural and religious expressions of such faith. The nurse cannot make any judgment about their inherent validity. As she writes in the introduction:

'Each culture expresses them [elementary human needs] differently and each individual in his own way. We do not offer them as a formula to explain human behaviour, which retains its mysterious qualities in spite of all that has been learned about it. As stated, these needs do not include specifically the common longing for a satisfying faith in a Higher Power or Ethic which serves man as a fixed point, or a guide to conduct. It does not specify his desire to live up to the demands of this faith so that he can feel "he walks in the light of God's countenance".'

(Henderson, 1969:7).

It is significant that Henderson uses inverted commas for this last statement, 'he walks in the light of God's countenance', for if as she argues the individual's need for some sort of higher power, ethic or god is beyond knowledge, God himself cannot be known. As for Kant, so for Henderson, God is merely an idea which grounds the voice of human conscience and so validates moral conduct (Kant, 1946).

An appraisal of sociocultural nursing approaches

The first issue to arise from this approach is the cultural problem. If beliefs and values are tied to and determined by religion and culture and are not defined by an objective truth, then it follows that it is not possible either to differentiate between belief systems on the grounds of truth or to bridge with genuine understanding differences in culture. From this relativist perspective, all religious belief systems from Judaism to Voodoo can claim equal validity. Hence the nurse has a responsibility to support her patient's belief system, unquestioningly, whatever it might be.

Yet because people themselves are constrained in these beliefs by their cultural background and heritage, the nurse herself is determined by her own cultural identity. Her own underlying values will govern the moral basis of her care. Indeed, Kant's whole rational philosophy was itself coloured by the Judaeo-Christian values derived from his sheltered Protestant upbringing and lifestyle (Warnock, 1964).

The logical implications of such an approach which denies knowledge of an underlying objective reality means that there is a gulf between, for example, the beliefs and values of the Free Presbyterian nurse from the Scottish Highlands and those of the Moslem patient from Bangladesh or indeed the Anglo-Catholic patient from Surrey, which makes the establishment of genuine relationships between cultures very difficult if not inherently impossible.

The second criticism is the materialistic Marxist criticism. If religion is deprived of its truth and viewed merely as a source of cohesiveness in society, and the idea of God is merely a validator for moral conduct, then it is open to Feuerbach's view that God is nothing more than a human projection (Küng, 1980). Indeed, this is exactly Henderson's view, as she writes:

'Humans endow the object of worship with the qualities they most admire. Religions are expressions of human values. People's values determine their purposes in life.'

(Henderson, 1978:1054)

When the idea of God is nothing more than projected human nature, then, as Marx and Freud argue (Küng, 1980), it is an idea which can be used as a sedative or opiate, a tool of oppression by the establishment to prevent the liberation of both the workers in society and the individual person; and, as feminists argue, it may be used as the source of oppression by the male establishment over women.

Indeed, Salvage (1985), Webb (1986) and Myco (1986) argue that religion has been used generally, and in nursing particularly, to suppress women and keep them subservient to men. For the patient then, religion, far from being a cohesive force that helps him cope with his powerlessness, is merely an institutional prop that prevents the transformation of power relations.

The third criticism is the existentialist criticism. This position seems to form the understanding of religion as expressed by the writer in *Mud and Stars*. Organised religion confuses and clouds the essential spirit of the human being — the authentic self. Human beings need to free themselves from such external constraints in order to be what they truly are, to empower themselves in striving for authenticity. Here is the clear message of Nietzsche (1974), which finds echoes in the Marxist, Freudian and feminist critiques of the existing order discussed above, and is the radical challenge to Kant. If there is no God, it is hypocritical to use the idea of God to validate human behaviour. The human being is free and it is this freedom that he must actualise.

Finally, there is the criticism of reductivism. Empiricist nurse theorists affirm the material and rational nature of the human being, and their clear focus on physical functioning make a vitally important contribution to patient care. Yet because they perceive nursing largely as a mechanistic process they tend to depersonalise the patient and reduce the practices of care into fragmented, compartmentalised functions. This opens an important dichotomy for nursing care and leads to dualism by splitting the science and art of nursing practice. The spiritual component of care is thus defined as an aspect of nursing practice application that is not integrated with other aspects of care.

The existential approach to the spiritual dimension of care

The philosophical basis

Nursing theories that take an existential perspective challenge mechanistic models of nursing care that reduce the human being to sets of systems. This is because existentialism protests against both rationalism and scientism. It is an ontological philosophy of existence directed towards the essence of living in the world in which the spiritual dimension is the lived experience of the individual, a discovery and self-actualisation of the authentic self in response to finitude.

Here is the spiritual 'I' of the *Mud and Stars'* writer, the area of growth of the real 'me', as I let go of systems, of body, mind and society, and grow into myself. This approach is clearly differentiated from sociocultural positions because it claims to disclose what Kant believed to be impossible, that is the underlying reality, the noumenon of human existence.

Macquarrie's analysis of existentialism clearly illustrates why existential philosophy has become attractive to nursing theorists. It safeguards many things that a pure empiricism loses from sight, including sympathy and love, the expression of the individual and personal character of each existence and 'the predominance of quality over quantity, of creativeness over adaptation' (Macquarrie, 1972:27).

Nursing writers using existentialist approaches draw on a wide spectrum of writers to develop their understandings of caring as ontological being, and, while the common thread is the focus on human experience, theories differ widely in the expression of that experience and thus the implications for patient care.

Existential nursing approaches that focus on the personal

Benner and her co-writer Wrubel (1989) provide a clear example of the existential nursing approach. They seek to redress Cartesian mind–body dualism through the use of existentialism and so develop a primary focus on holistic personal care. Benner and

Wrubel claim to use what they call a Heideggerian, hermeneutic methodology to build a philosophy of caring as concern, following Heidegger's (1962) concept of *Sorge* — a basic way of being in the world that creates both self and the world.

The expert nurse's narrative experience, the lived experience of everyday nursing, is the foundation and validator for expert nursing knowledge, independent of prescribed norms or formal models. It is this expert nurse who interprets the patient's experiences. The spiritual dimension of care is this lived experience. This is underlined by Benner (1991) in an article on what she calls 'ethical comportment'. In this article, she relates the narrative experience of a nurse caring for a young Amish boy, Sammy. The boy who had a severe brain injury was not expected to recover by the medical staff, but the faith of the family 'in their God, in Sammy and in us' (Benner, 1991:6) saw the unexpected miracle and the child recovered. The nurse describes how this incident caused her to examine herself. To quote Benner (1991:7):

'The experience doesn't turn the nurse into a believing Amish, but it does enlarge her moral imagination to include the possibilities she now recognizes in the Amish community. She translates their faith experience into her secular world but leaves room for the somewhat incommensurable world she has encountered.'

The appraisal of existential approaches that focus on the personal

Firstly, the use of Heidegger's (1962) understanding of care as a basis for a nursing theory of care needs to be questioned; Heidegger is not primarily concerned with care for others but rather care for self, for personal authenticity, for self-concern. His use of *Sorge* is akin to Kierkegaard's concept of *Angst* — anxiety (Macquarrie, 1972). This is a problem for nursing which is obviously concerned with others. The effect of using such an approach seems, inevitably, to result in the nurse focusing primarily on her own responses, feelings and experience.

This can be seen clearly in Benner. The narratives that she includes in her writings are those of the nurse rather than those of the patient. Indeed, the patient's experience is interpreted and given meaning by the nurse, and, as in the story of Sammy, it is not the child or the family's actualisation that is the nurse's focus, rather it is her own personal feelings. Moreover, the religious experience of the family is translated through, and contradicted by, the nurse's own viewpoint because it is coloured by the secular values used in her interpretation. This is inevitable since the phenomenological approach, by its nature, provides no independent means of assessing the nurse's interpretation of experience.

Furthermore, existential nursing approaches by virtue of their self-directed nature are predominantly concerned with self-actualisation and empowerment, not specifically for the cared-for but for the nurse herself and nursing generally. Indeed, Benner explicitly states that existential philosophy offers power to nurses, and it is this individualism and isolationism inherent in existentialism that poses severe problems for a practice discipline concerned with others. This seems to be an inevitable by-product of the use of Heideggerian philosophy for, as Macquarrie (1972) argues, Heidegger has very little to say about human relationships.

Secondly, because norms, structures and rules are rejected, the principles of scientific care become marginal to personal experience. This, too, is an inherent weakness in existential philosophy which, as Macquarrie also writes, has very little to say about the material body by which we have our being in the world. Indeed, Benner and Wrubel do try to remedy this by incorporating insights from Merleau-Ponty (1962), but he is interested in the body only as a tool of consciousness rather than as a material object in itself.

Thirdly, humanistic existentialism has no grounding to provide a moral framework for care. As Tillich (1967: 142) writes 'existentialism has no legs'. Each individual works out his or her own morality or way of living in the world in whichever way is authentic or 'true' for himself or for herself. This obviously poses severe problems for nursing: there can be no blueprint to guide the nurse's practice and provide objectively valid moral principles for care.

This lack of grounding causes difficulties for a philosophy concerned with the conscious experience of self-hood, for how does the individual self relate to the world in which he has his being? It is for this reason as we shall see that existentialist writers and thinkers have been driven to seek a grounding for the unattached self.

Existential nursing approaches that focus on the interpersonal

Paterson and Zderad (1976) seem to hold a similar position to Benner and Wrubel. They write that humanistic nursing practice is the existentially experienced nursing situation founded in the nurse's existential awareness of self and the other. Caring is a way of being in the world. Their difference, however, lies in Paterson and Zderad's stress on the existential grounding in relationality which they take from Buber and Marcel.

This is important because Macquarrie (1972) identifies both Buber (1970) and Marcel (1951) as the two existentialist writers who do develop an understanding of relationality. As Buber (1970:69) writes: 'In the beginning is the relation'. So human beings do not experience reality and truth alone but in the genuineness and mutuality of relationships. Both Buber, an orthodox Jew, and Marcel, a Roman Catholic, ground human relationality of the I and the Thou in the all-embracing, eternal Thou, God. Paterson and Zderad, however, do not acknowledge this grounding but instead focus, like Benner, on only one member of the caring relationship — the nurse who, using what Paterson and Zderad describe as a 'non-judgmental attitude', becomes the interpreter of the patient's experience.

Travelbee (1971), a lay Carmelite, is more consistent with existentialism in her approach. Drawing on Victor Frankl, she explicitly equates the spiritual dimension of the human being with his/her search for meaning in the face of illness, suffering and death. She focuses on the nursing relationship as the context for the sick person's self-actualisation. She sees the nurse as the agent that enables this authenticity, the growth of the patient's essential 'I'. Here Travelbee differs from Paterson and Zderad, for she suggests that the nurse must not remain neutral in the relationship. Instead she should bring her own beliefs and values to care — a non-judgmental attitude is indeed an impossible contradiction.

An appraisal of existential nursing approaches that focus on the interpersonal

The first question concerns the nature of the caring relationship. This is the criticism that Martin Buber levelled at Carl Rogers (Buber, 1990). The counselling relationship is not a genuine I/Thou relationship because the client has needs which the counsellor does not have. The two partners are not entering into a mutual relationship — the counsellor wants to hear all about the client but the client does not want to hear all about the counsellor. As Buber wrote to Rogers:

> '*You are, of course, a very important person for him [the sick person]. But not a person who he wants to see and to know and is able to. You're important for him... he is floundering around... He is, may I say, entangled in your life, in your thoughts, in your being, your communication, and so on. But he is not interested in you as you.*'

(Buber, 1990:49).

When transposed to the nursing situation, Buber's arguments maintain that the nurse–patient relationship is not an authentic personal relationship. The partners are not equal for the patient needs what he cannot give. This is one-sided care.

It is misguided for Travelbee to suggest that it is possible and desirable for the sick person to 'respond to the humanity of the nurse' and therefore perceive her not as a stereotype but as a person. Inevitably Buber's analysis raises the question of the effect and influence, however unintentional, of the nurse's own beliefs and values, whatever they may be, on the vulnerable patient's authentic search for meaning. Furthermore, this focus on the patient finding hope and meaning in suffering, which is undoubtedly a worthy counterbalance to theories of care that consider the patient merely as an ailing biological organism, in its turn undermines the scientific and physiological basis of care.

A primary focus on the patient's search for meaning in suffering may not only be ethically questionable, given the unequal nature of the nurse–patient relationship, and impractical for many patients and nurses within the time limitations of this relationship, but, significantly, may also mean that scientific alleviation and even cure of that suffering becomes a secondary consideration.

The second question concerns the grounding for both the relational and the personal. For Buber the guarantee of human relationality, its warmth, genuineness and mutuality lies in the all-embracing 'Thou'. For Frankl:

'Self-actualization is not man's ultimate destination. It is not even his primary intention. Self-actualization, if made an end in itself, contradicts the transcendent quality of human existence.'

(Frankl, 1964: 38)

His response to the question of ultimate meaning in the face of the existential vacuum is 'by trust in God' (Frankl, 1988:145).

Neither Paterson and Zderad nor Travelbee discuss this metaphysical grounding, although Travelbee, as a lay Carmelite, may presuppose it. However, the result of failing to ground these nursing theories is that the nursing relationship becomes inturned. The nurse becomes a self-consciously therapeutic tool for the self-actualisation of her patient using psychotherapeutic counselling techniques. Spiritual care is thus divided off from physical aspects of care and so becomes an external, or an external applied approach which separates off the personal and experiential from the physiological and so again leads to a dualism in care.

Existential nursing approaches that focus on the transpersonal

The issue then for existentialism is its grounding, the place of the individual existential self in the world of his existence. For Nietzsche (1974) and Sartre (1965) there is no ground but the self — total freedom and nothingness, the will to power, or the reason for despair (Macquarrie, 1972). For Kierkgaard (1941), Buber and Frankl there is the ground of a personal God. For Heidegger and

Maslow there is the ground of transpersonal, quasi-pantheism of a monistic world spirit. This is relevant to those nursing theories which use existential ideas, and it will be seen that some nursing writers, searching for a grounding for existentialism, take a similar route to Heidegger.

For Heidegger and Maslow, human being and becoming is reached through the disclosure of the universal world spirit or Hegelian *Geist*. This is not the personal God of the orthodox Judaeo-Christian tradition, but rather a mystical quasi-pantheism and monism in which human beings are not ultimately differentiated from the essence of creation. So, for Heidegger, being itself is the ground of existence and, as Macquarrie (1981) argues and Heidegger himself confirms, his philosophy shows clear similarities with Zen Buddhism.

For Maslow (1968; 1970; 1987) true integration for the individual, self-actualisation, involves the individual ascending a hierarchy of needs to reach his point of growth in being values that include, beauty, truth, goodness, justice, self-sufficiency, uniqueness and perfection. The final goal of self-actualisation is in the realms of the transcendent. The spiritual dimension of the human being reached through self-actualisation is ultimately a mystical experience, a letting-go of self, similar to Zen Buddhism. It is manifested in a form of love as detachment, an ego-transcendence, in which the individual loses himself by merging into the universal Nirvana.

Jean Watson seems to follow a similar path to Maslow and humanistic psychology. In early work which draws heavily on Carl Rogers and existential phenomenology, Watson suggests that individual experience is the foundation for understanding, and so the nurse turns 'inwards, to the self as the source of values and strengths' (Watson, 1985a:205). Yet it is not clear how she reconciles this belief which, like Benner, stresses human experience and 'gut level feeling' (Watson, 1985a:45) as fundamental for nursing understanding, with her assertion that scientific method and problem-solving techniques form nursing judgment.

Watson's position does, ultimately, favour existential phenomenology. This is clearly seen in her interpretation of the spiritual dimension of the human being as self-actualisation, a close parallel to Maslow's position, in which human fulfilment or what she calls 'god-likeness' are integrated with 'lower human needs' (Watson, 1985a:205).

It seems that in order to reconcile rational science with intuitive experience and find an ontological grounding for care in the foundations of the human essence, Watson takes a similar path to Heidegger and Maslow into Eastern mysticism (Watson, 1985b; 1987). Thus she sees caring itself as the moral essence of nursing in which care and love are universal and primal psychic energy. She believes that human beings are capable of transcending time and space through the universal spirit or essence which transcends the self to a higher degree of consciousness. Health is this harmony between mind, body and soul. The role of nursing is to actualise this caring consciousness.

So Watson suggests a paradigm shift for nursing, a metaphysical theory that goes beyond an existential-phenomenological perspective to a 'higher level of abstraction and sense of personhood, incorporating the concept of the soul and transcendence' (Watson, 1989:22). As she writes:

The further landscape that advances toward us bears little resemblance to what we have known before. Process, transcendence, transformation, emergence, patterns of relationships, relativity of time and space, non-physical phenomena, fluid energy fields all have implications for a new room for nursing science — as we seek new knowledge for new reasons.'

(Watson, 1989: 23).

This developing position which reaches for a grounding in a universal consciousness, an impersonal life-force which underpins creation, increasingly resembles the theory proposed by Martha Rogers (1970; 1980; 1989), and, through her influence, similar positions held by nurse theorists such as Parse (1989), Fitzpatrick (1983), Krieger (1981) and Quinn (1981).

Like Watson, Rogers claims that matter and spirit are indistinguishable. Existence is unitary and the human being is not separate from nature or from the universal spirit. This 'new science' which postulates a fourth dimension, is not empirically verifiable in Rogers opinion, rather it is experienced through the paranormal. Indeed, scientific understandings and norms such as average blood pressure readings will no longer be applicable as accelerating evolutionary changes, higher wave frequency patterns, 'manifest new norms for blood pressure readings'. Rogers (1980:335) spells out the implications of her spiritual understanding on patient care:

'Clairvoyance, for example, is rational in a four-dimensional environmental field. So too are events such as psychometry, therapeutic touch, telepathy and a wide range of other phenomena. Within this conceptual system such behaviors become "normal" rather than "paranormal".'

An appraisal of existential nursing approaches that focus on the transpersonal

The issues raised by both personal and interpersonal existentialism are further clarified by the strand of existentialism that finds its grounding in forms of monistic pantheism. Here both the personal and interpersonal become subordinated to the whole, which is itself impersonal. A life-force, which has no personality and therefore character, cannot be a moral force. It just is. It cannot care and therefore offers human beings no moral grounding for care. It is radically different from the Thou behind all Thous that is Buber's understanding of the personal God of Love.

In fact, as Mitchell (1980) points out, from the monistic perspective of Buddhism, for example, compassion is a form of asceticism and self-transcendence, an annihilation of desire that is primarily for the sake of the doer. This is because impersonal being underlying reality is experienced through the attunement of individual consciousness by detachment from self. From a monistic perspective, the human being has no more intrinsic worth than any creature. To quote Mitchell (1980: 127), man is merely 'a denizen of the earth, like an insect or an earthworm or a grass-snake.'

Yet not only does morality become relative, but conventional scientific principles are also undermined. This is because pantheism, by its very nature, sees physical phenomena of the material world as:

'an illusion whose existence is due merely to some unfortunate disturbance causing a temporary ripple on the surface of the eternal calm.'

(Garlick, 1943:93)

Such understandings parallel approaches to health in Eastern cultures such as China and India, where pantheistic religious beliefs focus on the energy balance of the ch'i, yin and yang and humours.

As Garlick points out, Buddhism for example, which stresses asceticism in the face of the cycle of punishing suffering that leads ultimately to a final absorption in the infinite, has produced a spirit of fatalism and inertia which was alien to the idea of scientific questioning and experiment. This approach also looks back to the Dark Ages of medieval Western society which tainted medicine with magic and astrology in place of observation and experiment. For practical nursing then, whose main focus is obviously assumed to be concerned with the physical health and care of the material body, this monistic, theoretical position raises many serious questions.

The covenant view of caring

The historic traditional approach to the spiritual dimension of care

We have seen that under the influence of modernity and without regard to tradition, nursing writers are trying to discover the spiritual heart of care. This is ironic as many nursing writers now assert that the very meaning of nursing care has become unclear. A backwards glance into nursing history reveals that the whole basis and development of care grew from its spiritual dimension. Indeed, it has been argued by the Greek nursing professor, Lanara (1976), and the Canadian sociologists, Hewa and Hetherington (1990), that the very reason for the twentieth century changes in nursing care, which undermined the personal aspects of caring, was due to the loss of this spiritual ethic. Certainly, a large number of British nurses, often hospital matrons, expressed their fears in the pages of nursing journals that as the spiritual basis of care was becoming marginal so nurses were being increasingly governed by a scientistic approach to care and, in the process, were losing what was so essential, the 'warmed heart' (e.g. Fox, 1912; Editorial, 1938; MacManus, 1956).

This spiritual tradition of care exemplified by this 'lamp tradition' of nursing rested on the biblical Judaeo-Christian principle of the covenant in which the image of light demonstrates the committed love of a personal and knowable God. Care for the sick was a moral imperative, a response to the divine call to love and thus a vocation to love one's neighbour as oneself. As Lord Walton (1990) argues, it was this idea of love that transformed Greek medicine from its concentration on *technie* to *anthropos*.

Here was the response of care by Christians in the Graeco-Roman world (Harnack, 1961), through the Middle Ages (Troeltsch, 1931), and famously revived by the inspired faith of Nightingale in the nineteenth century (Nightingale, 1860; 1873; 1882; Cook, 1913). Thus, as Troeltsch argues, periods of complacency, when the spiritual ideal was allowed to weaken, were followed by religious revivals and renewed spiritual activity. Yet even as late as the 1950s, this same spirit can be seen in the work of two women, Evelyn Pearce (1953) and Cicely Saunders, whose work was published in 1986.

Pearce, although virtually totally ignored by British nursing today, was a major influence on British nursing from the 1930s to the late 1960s through her *A General Textbook of Nursing* which reached 18 editions by 1969. She was an examiner for State Registration and her textbook was the core book used in nurse training. Although this text is largely focused on techniques, it alludes to the theological impetus and assumptions underlying what Pearce calls 'total patient care', which includes the spiritual dimension of the human being. Yet it is in a small book entitled

Nurse and Patient, written in 1953 and revised in 1959 and 1969, that Pearce (1953) makes her principles clear. This book stresses that in an age of materialism and scientific progress, people need to respond to the call for service and therein remember that 'patients are people' (Pearce, 1969:9). As she writes:

'It is the sincere wish of the author that this little book will be of use to those, who with faith in the supernatural and Divine destiny of man, have set out to minister to man's needs and to cherish him when he is sick.'

Pearce makes explicit the covenant basis of nursing at a time when this assumption was growing ever dimmer in the face of secular forces.

This was a similar motivation for Saunders (Du Boulay, 1984), who trained as a nurse, an almoner and a doctor in order to bring total patient care to those who were marginalised by the curative aims of medicine — the dying. In the 1960s, motivated by a strong Christian faith and with experience gained from the Christian foundations of St Joseph's Hospice and St Luke's Home, Saunders founded St Christopher's Hospice. She aimed to offer the dying both technical expertise, particularly in symptom control, and the compassion and security of a Christian foundation. Like Pearce, Saunders sought to care for the whole person in body, mind and spirit through the values and beliefs that compose the principles of covenant care.

It must be asked whether Nightingale, Pearce and Saunders sought to make explicit what many nursing writers themselves implicitly assume, but now explicitly reject. Henderson for example was, like Kant, brought up with the beliefs and values of a strong Protestant family, and although, as we have seen, she later rejected the claims of any one faith preferring a liberal humanism, Judaeo-Christian assumptions undoubtedly influenced her understanding of the nature of care (Smith, 1989). An analogy may therefore be drawn from Berkhof (1979), who suggests that the gospel fruit is picked from the gospel tree while the gospel tree is itself destroyed. This is precisely Nietzsche's argument; that the effects of the gospel tree will wear away over time once the tree has been (in his view rightfully) cut down.

Yet approaches to professional nursing are very different in cultures that are not influenced by the values of the Judaeo-Christian tradition, according to Meleis (1979; 1980) and Conduit (1986), who describe nursing in Muslim cultures and Chung-Tung (1991) and Chou Liu (1984), who describe nursing in China. The theological principles of this Judaeo-Christian approach to care as covenant, reiterated by Nightingale, Pearce and Saunders, need again to be made explicit not only in order to delineate the traditional spiritual nature of caring but also to clarify the principles of the tried-and-tested, common-sense tradition of nursing itself.

The covenant approach to care: implications for the patient

From a covenant understanding, the human being is both matter, composed of the same chemical substances as animals, and spirit, animated by the breath of God within. This is because human beings are created in the image and likeness of God, and creation itself reveals the nature of God as freedom and love. The destiny of the created human being is tied to God's free offer of covenant relationship which, even if rejected, is not withdrawn. So the uniqueness and value of the individual which differentiates him from the rest of creation is the personal love he is given by God.

For the patient, health is the strength to reflect this humanity, his/her createdness in the image of God, and to respond freely to the love offered by the covenant relationship. Human life therefore has an absolute value regardless of subjective judgments of worth or personal responsibility for illness. Physical and mental sickness are hindrances to covenant actualisation. The promotion of health and the removal of ill health are absolute priorities, both for the individual and for society. Yet because health is the strength to be human and thus to have a fulfilled relationship with God, it follows that a person with a frail and diseased body or mind may have such health, while the physically or mentally fit person may not. Thus the lines between sickness and health are blurred because the physical life of the organs and systems cannot be separated from the life of the soul.

From a covenant perspective, sickness, pain and death are real and not illusions. They are the result of chaos breaking into creation and thus are not ultimately under personal control. This contrasts with pantheistic positions which hold that spirit is undifferentiated from creation and therefore controllable through attunement to the cosmic energy force of universal consciousness. Although the inevitability of sickness and death confronts the individual with the reality of his finitude, covenant love — *agape* — offers the response.

This is clearly revealed through the paradigm of God's own incarnation; his identification with humanity in the suffering servant. The nature of this incarnation, the response of love in human relationships, offers help to the patient through the freedom of the heart in the face-to-face encounter; the commitment of love expressed through being cared for as a person. As Saunders (1987:4) writes:

> *'I once asked a man who knew he was dying what he needed above all in those who were caring for him. He said, "For someone to look as if they were trying to understand me".'*

The covenant approach to care: implications for the nurse

For the nurse, the theological understanding of creation emphasises the primary importance of science and technology both in the care of the sick and the prevention of disease. Thomas (1973) argues that historically it was the Judaeo-Christian tradition that laid the groundwork for the discoveries of natural science by asserting the fundamental material nature of creation. The vital importance of natural science as a foundation for nursing care was stressed by Nightingale (Cook, 1913), in her work on hygiene and disease prevention by Saunders (1986), in her work on symptom control and by Pearce (1967), in her textbook on nursing techniques, skills and procedures. This is the science of care, but creation needs to be held together with covenant. The science of creation must be integrated with the art of covenant love otherwise science gives way to scientism and nursing care becomes scientistic.

Covenant love is the response of the nurse to the covenant call, her moral response, her vocation. This was Nightingale's (Woodham-Smith, 1955) argument against Mrs Bedford Fenwick who sought to put nursing on a professional, scientific footing. Nightingale was afraid (and it seems rightly) that without the warmed heart of vocation, the nurse's care would become a mechanistic application of techniques, skills or knowledge. As Nightingale wrote to her probationers in 1888, a good nurse depends above all else on her moral character drawn from her covenant relationship with God. Body and soul for both nurse and patient are at one. Pearce's words echo Nightingale's 'Nursing is a spiritual service, the care of the soul can never be separated from the care of the body' (Pearce, 1969:79).

From a covenant perspective, as Pearce (1969) demonstrates, the nurse sees her patient as a person created in the image of God, loved by God and to whom she is called to respond in freedom and love. Using the paradigm exemplified by God himself and in the manner of the good Samaritan, she is called to any person who needs her of whatever race, creed or culture, with whatever health need or disease, however unattractive or even unresponsive.

This is not a contractual duty but a covenant service, nor is it a detached self-denial; rather it is because the nurse is herself created in love and for love that she is able to reflect that love to others. As a nurse, whether she knows it or not, she is fulfilling her own createdness by this commitment which asks for neither satisfaction nor return because it does not depend on the capriciousness and fallibility of personal human feelings and sentiments but on the steadfastness of covenant love.

This is the nature and definition of love as *agape* and the ground for the equality of the nurse–patient relationship which safeguards the intimacy of the relationship against any manipulation, however unintentional. It is manifested in the genuineness of the nurse's moral character and expressed through her warmed heart; in the devotion, skill, patience, gentleness, sensitivity, sympathy and compassion with which she encounters the patient, meets him eye to eye and face to face, listens to his words and fears, truthfully explains and answers him. All this is performed with an unselfconscious gladness governing every action; whether the nurse is cleaning away excreta, making pillows comfortable, ensuring that drinks are in reach, or performing complex technical procedures.

Yet, in this covenant service, the nurse herself is not an autonomous, isolated individual seeking personal empowerment, but a limited human being who is also in complementary relationships with her colleagues and with whom care needs to be shared in a spirit of mutual cooperation.

According to Saunders (1986), the trust, peace and hope of care, its security for the vulnerable patient, depend on this covenant foundation which preserves both the personhood of the individual in need of care and the nature of the community in which such care is given expression. Yet the carer does not express the covenant foundation verbally or self-consciously, rather she offers it practically through service, in the freedom of her heart through the action of *agape*, grounded love.

This pastoral model of nursing, the model underpinning the now fractured lamp tradition of nursing, I suggest, is uniquely the spiritual dimension of caring, the dignity and comfort of care. It is our common-sense heritage which we need to hold in trust.

References

Ayer A (1978) Logical positivism and its legacy. In: Magee B, ed. *Men of Ideas*. Oxford University Press, Oxford

Benner P (1991) The role of experience, narrative and community in skilled ethical comportment. *Adv Nurs Sci* **14**: 1–21

Benner P, Wrubel J (1989) *The Primacy of Caring*. Addison-Wesley, California

Berkhof H (1979) *An Introduction to the Study of the Christian Faith*. Eerdmans, Grand Rapids, Ohio

Buber M (1970) *I and Thou*. T & T Clark, Edinburgh

Buber M (1990) Carl Rogers: Dialogues. In: Kirschenbaum H, Henderson V, eds. *Buber*. Constable, London

Chou Liu Y (1984) China: traditional healing and contemporary medicine. *Intl Nurs Rev* **31(4)**: 110–14

Chung-Tung L (1991) From san gu liu po to 'caring scholar': the Chinese nurse in perspective. *Intl J Nurs Stud* **28**: 315–24

Conduit N (1986) Culture clash. *Nurs Times* **82(49)**: 19–20

Cook E (1913) *The Life of Florence Nightingale*. Macmillan, London

Du Boulay S (1984) *Cicely Saunders*. Hodder Stoughton, London

Durkheim E (1915) *The Elementary Forms of Religious Life*. George Allen & Unwin, London

Editorial (1938) The warmed heart. *Nurs Times* **xxxiv(1727)**: 579

Fitzpatrick J (1983) A life perspective model. In: Fitzpatrick J, Whall A, eds. *Conceptual Models of Nursing*. Prentice-Hall, London

Fowler J (1981) *Stages of Faith*. Harper Row, San Francisco

Fox M (1912) Nursing ethics. *Nurs Times* **8**: 475–8

Frankl V (1964) *Man's Search for Meaning*. Hodder Stoughton, London

Frankl V (1988) The Will to Meaning. Merdian, New York

Garlick P (1943) *The Wholeness of Man*. Highway Press, London

Goodrich A (1932) *The Social and Ethical Significance of Nursing*. Macmillan, New York

Harnack A (1961) *The Mission and Expansion of Christianity in the First Three Centuries*. Harper Torchbooks, New York

Heidegger M (1962) *Being and Time*. SCM, London

Henderson V (1969) *Basic Principles of Nursing Care*. International Council of Nurses, Geneva

Henderson V (1978) Worship. In: Henderson V, Nite G, eds. *Principles and Practice of Nursing*. 6th edn. Macmillan, New York

Hewa S, Hetherington R (1990) Specialists without spirit: crisis in the nursing profession. *J Med Ethics* **16**: 179–84

James W (1960) *The Varieties of Religious Experience*. Fontana, Glasgow

Kant I (1946) *Fundamental Principles of the Metaphysic of Ethics.* Longman Green , London

Kant I (1977) Prolegomena to any future metaphysic. In: Cahn S, ed. *Classics of Western Philosophy.* Hackett, Indianapolis

Kierkegaard S (1941) *Training in Christianity.* Oxford University Press, London

Krieger D. ed (1981) *Foundations of Holistic Health Nursing Practices.* Lippincott, Philadelphia

Küng H (1980) *Does God Exist?* Collins, London

Lanara V (1976) Philosophy of nursing and current nursing problems. *Intl Nurs Rev* 23: 48–54

McManus E (1956) *Matron of Guy's.* Andrew Melrose, London

Macquarrie J (1972) *Existentialism.* Penguin, Harmondsworth

Macquarrie J (1981) *Twentieth Century Religious Thought.* SCM, London

Marcel G (1951) *The Mystery of Being.* Gateway, Chicago

Maslow A (1968) *Towards a Psychology of Being.* Von Nostrand Reinhold, New York

Maslow A (1970) *Motivation and Personality,* 2nd edn. Harper Row, New York

Maslow A (1987) *Motivation and Personality. Revised by Frager R, Fradiman J, McReynolds C, Cox R. Harper Collins, New York*

Meleis A (1979) International issues in nursing education: the case of Kuwait. *Intl Nurs Rev* 26(4): 107–10

Meleis A (1980) A model for establishment of educational programmes in developing countries: the nursing paradoxes in Kuwait. *J Adv Nurs* 5: 285–300

Merleau-Ponty M (1962) *Phenomenology of Perception.* Routledge Kegan Paul, London

Mitchell B (1980) *Morality: Religious and Secular.* Oxford University Press, Oxford

Myco F (1985) The non-believer in the health care situation. In: McGilloway O, Myco F eds. *Nursing and Spiritual Care*. Harper Row, London

Nietzsche F (1974) *The Gay Science*. Vintage Books, New York

Nightingale F (1860) *Suggestions of Thought to the Searchers after Truth among the Artisans of England* (3 vols). Eyre Spottiswode, London

Nightingale F (1873) *Letters and addresses to Probationer Nurses in the `Nightingale Fund' School at St Thomas's Hospital and Nurses who were formerly trained there*. Original letters and prints for private circulation held by University College, London

Nightingale F (1882) Nursing the sick. In: Quain R, ed. *A Dictionary of Medicine*. Part II. Longmans Green, London

Parse R (1989) Man-living health: a theory of nursing. In: Riehl-Sisca J, ed. *Conceptual Models for Nursing Practice*. Appleton Lange, Norwalk

Paterson J, Zderad L (1976) *Humanistic Nursing*. John Wiley, New York

Pearce E (1953) *Nurse and Patient*. 1st edn. Faber & Faber, London

Pearce E (1967) *A General Textbook of Nursing*. 17th edn. Faber & Faber, London

Pearce E (1969) *Nurse and Patient*. 3rd edn. Faber & Faber, London

Quinn J (1981) Client care and nurse involvement in a holistic framework. In: Krieger D, ed. *Foundations for Holistic Health Nursing Practices*. Lippincott, Philadelphia

Rogers M (1970) *An Introduction to the Theoretical Basis of Nursing*. F A Davis, Philadelphia

Rogers M (1980) Nursing: a science of unitary man. In: Riehl J, Roy C, eds. *Conceptual Models for Nursing Practice*. Appleton-Century-Crofts, New York

Rogers M (1989) Nursing: a science of unitary human beings. In: Riehl-Sisca J, ed. *Conceptual Models for Nursing Practice*. Appleton Lange, Norwalk

Salvage J (1985) *The Politics of Nursing*. Heinemann, London

Sartre J-P (1965) *Existentialism and Humanism*. Methuen, London

Saunders C (1986) The modern hospice. In: Wald F, ed. *In Quest of the Spiritual Component of Care for the Terminally Ill*. Yale University Press, New Haven

Saunders C (1987) I was sick and you visited me. *Christian Nurse Intl* 3(4): 4, 5

Smith J (1989) *Virginia Henderson: The First Ninety Years*. Scutari, Harrow

Thayer H (1964) Pragmatism. In: O'Connor D, ed. *A Critical History of Western Philosophy*. Free Press of Glencoe, New York

Thomas K (1973) *Religion and the Decline of Magic*. Penguin, Harmondsworth

Tillich P (1967) *Perspectives in Nineteenth and Twentieth Century Protestant Theology*. SCM, London

Travelbee J (1971) *Interpersonal Aspects of Nursing*. F A Davis, Philadelphia

Troeltsch E (1931) *The Social Teaching of the Christian Churches*. Vols 1 and 2. George Allen & Unwin, London

Walton J (1990) *Method in Medicine*. 1990 Harveian Oration of the Royal College of Physicians, London

Warnock G (1964) Kant. In: O'Connor D, ed. *A Critical History of Western Philosophy*. Free Press of Glencoe, New York

Watson J (1985a) *Nursing: The Philosophy and Science of Caring*. Colorado Association University Press, Colorado

Watson J (1985b) *Nursing: Human Science and Human Care*. National League for Nursing, New York

Watson J (1987) Nursing on the caring edge: metaphorical vignettes. *Adv Nurs Sci* 10: 10–18

Watson J (1989) Watson's philosophy and theory of human caring. In: Riehl-Sisca J, ed. *Conceptual Models for Nursing Practice*. Appleton Lange, New York

Webb C (1986) *Feminist Practice in Women's Health Care*. John Wiley, Chichester

Weber M (1965) *The Sociology of Religion*. Methuen, London

Woodham-Smith   C   (1955)   *Florence   Nightingale.*   Penguin,
    Harmondsworth

Working Party (1991) *Mud and Stars.* Sobell Publications, Oxford

Chapter 2

Art, caring, spirituality and humanity

Jean Watson

Dominant world-view assumptions and mindsets, unexamined, can and do influence the very foundation of nursing practice, in that they shape our views toward self, other and to humanity itself. This chapter explores the connections between the caring, art and spirituality, and how we are called to reconnect these dimensions into our most personal and professional heartfelt practices.

Art, caring, spirituality and humanity

After his first trip to Colorado, USA, my Scots colleague Dr Philip Dabyshire wrote to me the following:

'Hilary is reading Bury My Heart at Wounded Knee *just now and it struck me how depressingly familiar that story is of the elimination of entire peoples and cultures — from North American Indians, Aboriginals, Highlanders, to today's "ethnic cleansing in Bosnia". If ever the world cried out for Human Caring.'*

(Darbyshire, 1992)

You may wonder what Philip's troubling and compassionate comments have to do with the topic of art in nursing and caring.

To the extent that his comments reflect abuse and misuse of human spirit and humanity worldwide, and to the extent he indicated that the world is crying out for human caring, we can begin to make some links to the role of art and caring.

First let us explore how our caring or lack of caring is related to our view of humanity and how we attend to the concept of human spirit in the midst of this everyday 'Madonna's material world'.

Heidegger (1962) helped us to see that our age is the first whose paradigm is a work, not of art, but of technology. Being a technologic construct, the world we have tried to create is value-free. As philosopher Houston Smith framed it:

> *'Quite irrevocably, something enormous has happened to Western
> Man (sic). His outlook on life and the world has changed so
> radically ...it is as if, standing before a picture window that opens
> on to an alpine landscape, we ...lowered the shade to the point
> where we can now see little more than the ground at our feet.'*

(Smith, 1984: xiii)

It is ironic that, while at the height of twentieth century medical successes, our advanced biomedical science and technology alone cannot relieve the contemporary crisis of caring and the oppressed human spirit in the modern health-care system. There is also increasing uncertainty as to whether even logic or moral reason, as constructed by current thinking, can get much further than science in solving the issues.

As T S Eliot said:

> *'It leaves me with no idea where truth lies, save that it must be in
> the opposite direction from here.'*

(cited by Smith, 1984: 167)

The twentieth century has been identified as post-modern in that it is an era influenced by 'modernism' that had a mindset that was characterised as shapeless; it represented a loss of faith in any higher order other than human order and control.

The dominant assumptions of an age colour the thoughts, beliefs, expectations and images of the men and women who live within — but these assumptions usually pass unnoticed because they are so often with us, they stop being observed and we no longer see. This does not mean that they have no affect — indeed, they refract the world in ways that condition our very being, our art and our institutions, our degrees of caring and compassion toward self and others; these dominant assumptions shape our criteria for caring, for being human.

For example, how our world-view and dominant assumptions about life, nature, humans and the universe influence our reality and our acts with respect to the human spirit, can be illustrated in the development of the theory of evolution itself. Bronowski (1973), in his work *The Ascent of Man*, wrote about how the theory of natural selection was put forward in the 1850s independently by two men — one was Charles Darwin, the other was Alfred Russell Wallace. Both men had some scientific background, of course, although at heart both men were naturalists.

Darwin, however, had been a medical student at Edinburgh University for 2 years before he was sent to Cambridge by his wealthy father doctor. Wallace, on the other hand, had poor parents and had left school at 14-years-old; he had followed courses at Working Men's Institutes in London and other places as an apprentice. He remained an astute naturalist, lived in the wild as a land surveyor and eventually became a full-time naturalist. He remained committed, as Bronowski put it:

'to the study of the processes of life; their delicacy, their diversity, the wavering cycles from life to death in the individual and in the species.'

(Bronowski, 1973: 291).

Bronowski indicated that Wallace's view and explanation of the ascent of the human marched side-by-side as one of two traditions of explanation of humans and life processes. Darwin represented the modern tradition which was an analysis of the physical structure of the world, leading to the theory of evolution.

Upon encountering peoples that were foreign to their ways, Darwin and Wallace had markedly different perceptions and responses to those 'others'. Bronowski described Darwin, upon meeting the natives of Tierra del Fuego in South America, as horrified (p 303). He said that this was clear from Darwin's own words as well as from the drawings in his book. Wallace, on the other hand, was reported as having a rare sympathy with their culture, in an age in which Victorians called the people of the Amazon 'savages' (Bronowski, 1973: 301).

In contrast to the 'horror' that Darwin experienced, Wallace was reported to be both excited and frightened when, for the first time, he went into the native Indian village. He wrote:

'The ...most unexpected sensation of surprise and delight was my first meeting and living with a man in a state of nature... They were all going about their own work or pleasure which had nothing to do with white men or their ways; they walked with the free step of the independent forest dweller and ...in every detail they were original and self-sustaining... who could and did live their lives in their own way, as they had done for countless generations before America was discovered.'

(Bronowski, 1973: 300)

Bronowski indicated that Wallace understood what language, what invention, what custom meant to them. Wallace was perhaps the first person to seize the fact that the cultural distance between an indigenous civilisation and ours is much shorter than we think; that we are after all part of the human race with many manifestations of life, its expressions, its forms and its diversity.

What I want to illustrate from this example is how one's point of view, one's dominant assumptions affect one's very real view of life, nature and human existence — one's sense of caring, compassion and connectedness with humanity in all its various forms and one's relationship to nature and life's processes.

Our so-called 'modern scientific assumptions and world-view about humanity' has tainted our openness to what it means to be human, what it means to engage the human spirit through our nursing arts. As Laing (1965) reminded us years ago, we can choose to see 'other' as different from self and without other doing anything differently. We can also choose to see other as another human being not unlike self in that we share common human conditions. However, in the example, due to two different perceptions and mindsets, Wallace and Darwin saw the 'other' very differently. One saw 'other' as an enemy, the second man saw 'other' as a curious human whom he was eager to learn more about.

As quoted by McIntyre (1993), Kristeva (1990), a French philosopher and psychoanalyst, points out:

'We see the other as enemy when we project the "strangeness within" of our own unconscious to the exterior and scapegoat them on to others.'

(McIntyre, 1993: 27)

Indeed, according to Kristeva and McIntyre, it is the refusal to see the other as enemy that forms the basis for morality. They conclude that in the current world 'we lack the moral code that permits us to think of the other' (p27). For example, it is when one is able to see and hear the other like self that one can refuse to see other as enemy. Some of these same dynamics hold true for us in nursing, in our mindset, our perceptions and our choices related to our views of self and other. These affect our very view of what it means to be human and how we engage or disengage from the caring-healing arts that connect with, nourish, liberate and unify the human mindbodyspirit.

Consequently, our assumptions and knowledge can have 'morally disturbing' consequences; what Nel Noddings (1989) reveals as the 'real evils' in society; what Ernest Gellner, a philosopher and sociologist refers to as '...the inescapable price of Faustian purchase of real knowledge, ...which exacts its inherent moral, 'dehumanising' price ...that our identities, freedom, norms are no longer underwritten by our vision and comprehension of things...' (Gellner; in Smith, 1984: 78).

Darwin and Wallace left us with a long legacy of human evolution which still dominates our unconscious assumptions about who and what is worthy of caring and preserving in humanity, be it human or animal or any living thing, including nature herself. Indeed, even the shape of our knowledge and the eco-crisis of nature and our environment has been influenced from such assumptions that separate us rather than connect, reminding us that the shape of our thinking and approaches to knowing can form or deform the human soul (Parker, 1987; Watson, 1990).

Noddings (1989) insists that all actual epistemologies and moralities are created from and represent standpoints. She reframes Evil from a standpoint of fictionalised Evil and women with stories of defilement, horror and bewitchment, to the realisation of evil as real and something that must be faced. She faces it from a standpoint of that of women. The real evils that she unveils are not women and evil in the oldest theological and philosophical perspectives, but human pain, poverty, war and torture largely perpetuated by men for control and domination over nature, others and, ultimately, those they love including one's own humanity.

These moral issues embodied in Darwin and Wallace's experiences as well as in Noddings' treatment of evil are paralleled modern science, leading us to an era that is in competition with evolution, and is anti-survival rather than co-operative, caring, compassionate and artistic. All of these discussions are linked to suppression and oppression of the human spirit, now resulting in spiritual longings which call out to be filled.

One way to foster the reversal of oppression, evil and anti-survival practices, to reconnect us with caring and the evolution of the human spirit is through use of caring-healing arts in education and clinical practices.

A case for arts and caring

Bronowski considered the arts as either expressing or transmitting human knowledge. Indeed, he goes on to propose that the arts are a most important carrier of knowledge. From them we derive an insight into human experience and, through that, into human values which makes the arts one of the fundamental modes of human knowledge. He pointed out that although science and art share in their modes something of predictive and practical value, the mode of knowledge of science is explanatory. Art carries knowledge that is profound but in the end is not offered as an explanation.

To the extent that art is one expression of the human spirit and a means of access to the human soul, and to the extent that the caring praxis is an art, perhaps then we can locate arts and caring together as a means of informing nursing in its collective, global, moral mission of preservation of human dignity, human integrity and preservation of humanity worldwide. The province of art is an intensification and clarification of human experiences; those experiences may be intensified, heightened or dulled and obscured; they may remain painful, brutal, dim and chaotic; art may help them become meaningful and clear and alive; may indeed lead to social action based upon both art and ethics of caring.

A reconnection of caring with spirituality and art is called for during such a tumultuous, cataclysmic world-view change. During a time of transition from one century to another, during a time of shifting cultural, moral, scientific and political forces, forward steps must be taken by nursing to sustain human caring in instances of threatened humanity — biological or otherwise.

It has been rhetorically asked 'What are the human conditions that *collectively* facilitate and sustain the preservation of humanity in instances of threatened humanity? (Watson, 1988)' and further, 'Nursing has been posited as a human science with caring as the moral foundation — a foundation which is always threatened and fragile. It is so threatened because human caring requires a personal, social, moral and spiritual engagement of the nurse and commitment to oneself and others' (Watson, 1988).'

Preservation of humanity at the highest level is the ultimate end of nursing's caring in society. That preservation-end includes connecting with the humanity of self and the other toward the goal of protection of the spiritual, the soul of a person or of a peoples, and, ultimately, preservation of the collective soul of humankind which we are perilously close to destroying.

However, nursing cannot get there from here, in spite of our commitment to caring and to art and preservation of humanity in society. We have been blinded by our world-view.

Again, as Laing (1965) put it, 'It is like trying to make ice by boiling water.' Edgar Allen Poe, in his Sonnet to Science, provides us with some poetic insight to our dilemma:

'Science! True daughter of Old Time thou art.
Who alterest all things with thy peering eyes.
Why preyest thou thus upon the poet's heart,
Vulture, whose wings are dull realities?
...Who wouldst not leave him in his wandering to seek for
treasure in the jewelled skies;
...To seek a shelter in some happier star?'

(Galloway, 1980)

Something new is required, both in science and art, for our views of caring.

Concerning the spiritual in caring and art

The reason that the modern Western world of science and its views of humanity and nature are inadequate is precisely because Western science does not accommodate values and ethics of caring; nor does it accommodate the human soul or human spirit or art in its paradigm. In the most specific sense, the dominant model of science has eliminated or sought to control and dominate the human spirit. Yet it is notions of art and spirituality and preservation of humanity, which is the heart of nursing's finest view of itself and its role and mission worldwide. This vision holds even in the midst of dramatic practice changes, new knowledge and technology.

A model incorporating the arts and humanities can be used by nurses to connect caring with preservation of humanity and fostering spirituality and the evolution of the human spirit in a global sense. The art of nursing in the broadest sense allows nursing to come of age during this post-modern era, to reconnect with the finest of our history and tradition while also fostering and clarifying caring–healing arts.

As Nightingale (1952) put it: *'Nursing activities are the art from which patients are enabled to spiritually develop.'*

Art is the essence of life's spirit. Art captures, expresses and recreates humanity and life itself — in all its various forms. Art mirrors the human soul.

Thomas Moore (1992), in his book *Care of the Soul* , points out that art is one form of care of the soul. It allows the act of entering into the mysteries of the soul, encouraging life to blossom forth according to its own design and own unpredictable beauty. Art and the soul are linked through the sacred nature of both, which connect with higher human purposes.

The metaphor of the human heart as a machine body part, as an object for medical study and treatment, versus the heart as the metaphysical seat of the soul is one way to consider the spiritual in our world of contemporary medical practices. If the heart is the metaphorical and symbolic seat of the soul and we do not concern ourselves with the spiritual, then we reduce ourselves and those we care for to the literal level of machine — a pump of sorts to convey and carry out objective regimes. We become a throw-away nurse — efficient, easily replaceable — thereby directing us toward the mechanical, the technicalities of our work, not art; no heart, no meaning.

Indeed, this 'no life, no heart' phenomenon is more prevalent than we might imagine. As part of a nationally commissioned task force in the USA which is studying the need for psychosocial medical education reform, a survey was conducted among different medical schools on how they introduce first-year medical students to 'the cadaver and autopsy experience'. This experience seems to be a barometer for medical education and anything 'concerning the spiritual' in caring or curing. It was reported that one very prominent, well-established, nationally ranked medical school introduced its first-year medical students to this experience by the professor writing on the chalkboard two words: *Dead Mammal.* This was the beginning orientation to medical education. Another medical school with a stated philosophy of commitment to their community, to values-based education and whole-person learning, introduced their students to the same experience with a candlelight memorial service designed to have the students honour the gift of life and the gift that these individuals and families gave by allowing their bodies to be used for the students' learning the mysteries of life. These are examples of two dramatically different orientations to life and to the spiritual in our professional practices.

Just as the human heart captures life's spirit and spirituality, art and nature combine. As Emerson (1982) said:

'Nature is the symbol of the spirit. ...Nature always wears the colours of the spirit. Art conspires with the spirit in search of beauty, wisdom and truth' (p48).

This truth that Emerson and others speak is not a scientific truth as we like to pursue, but an inner truth.

It is art which conspires with the human spirit to emancipate us. Such art which comes from our heartfelt practices can be likened to the thinking of Friere (1971), Maxine Greene (1990)and Nel Noddings (1989) as they, as educators, write of freedom and emancipatory learning that emancipates the human spirit. The art of caring pedagogies and practices allows us to locate ourselves in another space and place that change in our perceptions, our way of seeing and being. Art and the spiritual shifts our relations of parts and whole.

Concerning the spiritual within the art of nursing throws a light upon the mystery of humanity. It preserves the mystery rather than seeking to control and order it. The final link between caring, art and the human spirit is for beauty itself:

'The world thus exits to the soul to satisfy the desire of beauty.
...No reason can be asked or given why the soul seeks beauty.
Beauty, in its largest and profoundest sense is an expression for the universe .'

(Emerson, 1982: 47, 48).

May this era between centuries be the turning-point whereby nursing restores and further develops its caring–healing art and spiritual dimensions lest the profession collectively dies of a broken heart.

References

Bronowski J (1973) *The Ascent of Man*. Little Brown, Boston

Dabyshire P (1992) Personal correspondence from Glasgow, Scotland

Emerson RW (1982) *Selected Essays*. Penguin, Middlesex

Friere P (1971) *Pedagogy of the Oppressed*. Herder, New York

Galloway D ed (1980) *Selected Writings of Edgar Allan Poe*. Penguin, Hansworth

Greene M (1990) The Tension and Passions of Caring. In: Leininger M, Watson J eds. *The Caring Imperative in Education*. NLN, New York: 29–44

Heidegger M (1962) *Being and Time*. SCM Press, London

Laing RD (1965) *The Divided Self*. Penguin, Middlesex

McIntyre M (1993) *Constituting Understanding: The Meaning of being Understood in Illness*. PhD Dissertation, University of Colorado School of Nursing

Moore T (1992) *Care of the Soul*. Harper Collins, New York

Nightingale F (1952) *Notes on Nursing: What it is and What it is not*, 4th edn. Duckworth, London

Noddings N (1989) *Women and Evil*. University of California, Berkely

Parker P (1987) Community, conflict and ways of knowing. *Mag H Educ* **19**: 20–5

Smith H (1984) *Beyond the Postmodern Mind*. First Quest Theosophical, New York

Watson J (1988) *Nursing Human Science and Human Care*. NLN, New York

Watson J (1990) The Moral Failure of the Patriarchy. *Nursing Outlook* **38**(2): 62–6

Chapter 3

A ministry of healing

by David Lunan

As a contribution to the debate on the spiritual dimension in caring, I will share a little of what I have learned and experienced about the spirituality of caring in 25 years of pastoral work. By profession, ministers live every day with matters spiritual, which in itself can be harmful to the spirit for it is hard to wrestle continuously with ultimate questions. It is easier and indeed necessary sometimes to avoid exploring deep, holy and ultimate issues. The danger, however, is that we become detached and professional, developing techniques for fitting life's rich and varied pattern into a manageable package, and losing much of the sense of mystery in the process. To provide a back-drop for this brief account of my ministry, I first have to say a little about my approach to life.

I believe in God; that he is the ultimate reality. I believe that God is a spirit; that Jesus is the visible likeness of that invisible reality — the human face of God. I believe that the Spirit of God is at work in the world. The one word which sums up any description of this ultimate spiritual reality is *love*. Any genuine experience of love is an authentic experience of God. Love can be expressed in words but more often it is expressed in deeds. I believe that, whatever other powers are operating in the world around, the most potent, the most enduring, the most creative, the most healing is *love*.

The title of this book includes the word 'exploring', which is of critical importance since it denotes humility before the immense mysteries of human relationships and of the human psyche: the mysteries of the meaning and purpose of life, the whys and the wherefores of suffering and evil and the absence of caring. When we are dealing in spiritual things, it is wise to heed the words of the Trappist monk, Thomas Merton who said:

'We do not want to be beginners, but let us be convinced of the
fact that we will never be anything else but beginners all our life.'

It is therefore right that people should instinctively beware of anyone who claims to be an expert in the realm of the spirit. In any spiritual quest, we are raising questions, knocking on doors, looking around us with inquiring eyes but, even more important, we are looking inwards and searching our own hearts. We are simply explorers, but whatever dangers lie in the path, the exploration, the adventure is worthwhile.

Spirituality

The word spirituality has become something of a buzz-word and can mean all things to all people. It is not a word that is always tackled in church circles, sometimes being neatly wrapped in pious nostrums, but more often abandoned in vague and meaningless platitudes. Sometimes, it helps to think of spiritual as being all that is non-material. So, using this definition, we are exploring all the non-material aspects of caring. Yet Christianity, as Archbishop Temple (1938) once said, is the most avowedly materialist of all great religions. Jesus was concerned for peoples bodies' as well as their souls, and how we approach all these things says something about our spirituality. Charles Peguy, the French mystic, says everything begins in piety and ends in politics. A Swiss theologian expresses it like this:

'Bread for me is a material question, bread for my neighbour is a
spiritual question'.

(Merton, 1973)

Thus, in reflecting on the term 'spiritual' (beside there being in us and around us continually a realm of spiritual existence), I like to use the words 'attitude' and 'atmosphere'. They reflect something of the internal and external aspects of all that is spiritual. We say of someone that he has the right attitude, the right spirit: we say of a place or an event that 'the atmosphere was good', meaning the spirit was good. So I use the word to encompass all that comprises our world-view: upbringing, training, experience, temperament, imagination, as well as mood, environment and culture.

Caring

From a Christian standpoint, the purpose of our caring is for the benefit of the other person. It is not concerned with status or self-gratification. Caring is concerned with assisting the one cared for towards a better quality of life, more freedom, more contentment, more sense of worth and of meaning, more peace of mind, more healing. Sometimes that cannot be afforded satisfactorily without some personal cost to the one who is caring. More often, there is a mutuality in our caring, but it is not guaranteed. So it is important, indeed essential, that the person who is caring knows both how to sustain and protect him/herself; knows that he/she is cared for and valued, and that he/she retains a certain quality of life and general wholesomeness. Otherwise, the caring becomes a form of condescension, or a meeting of the carer's own insecurities, inadequacies or needs. These are ultimately spiritual issues that require to be explored.

The power of prayer

What I now want to explore is one aspect of caring spiritually for others; healing through prayer. I personally regard all ministry as healing. I view the church as an agency for healing in the world; being concerned with the ailments of the individual soul, with social sores, and the healing and health of nations. The church has not found it easy to come to terms with the healing part of Christ's ministry and has contrived different ways of explaining it away. The liberal wing say that miracles probably never happened, or, if they did, that there is a perfectly rational explanation in terms of first century diagnostic limitations; the conservative wing say that Jesus was God so of course it was quite possible for him to act in sovereign power. But we are not God, and so those incidents are consigned to history, for apostolic times only. I am convinced not only that some of the gospel accounts are accurate in detail, but also that what happened then can happen now.

Nevertheless, people do have legitimate questions about the ministry of healing. Does not God heal primarily through normal methods — the body's own recuperative powers; the intellectual acumen of physicians; the skilled hands of surgeons; the sensible tenderness of nurses; the discoveries of drug researchers, and so on? The answer is emphatically yes. If I am sick, I go to the doctor. If I have toothache, I go to the dentist. A ministry of healing is not in any way an alternative or a competitor, but lies alongside conventional practices. I believe that when the Church properly fulfils its function of putting people in touch with God, the ultimate spiritual reality of love, then these people are given a sense of their own worth, a source of strength and a desire to be a reflection of, or a channel of the love that they have discovered in life.

Some Christian people believe that illness is a 'cross to bear', and therefore imagine that it would be wrong to seek to have this cross removed. This is not helpful. I think that what happened at some stage in Christian history is that when general persecution ceased, the suffering associated with being out of step with the rest of the world became transferred in people's minds with the suffering associated with illness. But the fact is that Jesus never saw illness as a blessing in disguise; he saw it as an affliction to be overcome. He never said to a sick person 'That is your cross to bear'; he healed them. There are others who look upon this whole area of healing as decidedly weird. There is indeed an aspect of spiritual healing that attracts people who we might consider as odd. Healing through prayer can be slightly controversial, but then our Lord was more than a little controversial; and even he was accused of healing people by black magic, by the power of the devil.

It is important to note at this point that the Greek word for health is also the Greek word for salvation. The original Greek word is translated in the bible as Jesus saves, and as Jesus heals. Even in English there is a linguistic connection between holiness and wholeness. Jesus makes holy; Jesus makes whole, complete, well-rounded, wholesome, healthy. For me, healing is about creating or restoring wholesomeness. People can be perfect physical specimens but spiritually adrift; others can be ill or handicapped, but as persons they are giants, exhibiting all the human qualities that we long for.

Jesus used different methods to heal: sometimes he met the person, sometimes he did not; sometimes he touched the person, sometimes he did not; sometimes it was the power of his words that brought healing, on other occasions he used spittle. So there were different approaches. Nowhere, incidentally, do we read of him praying with sick people.

The key is faith: sometimes the faith of the patient; sometimes of the patient's friends or family; sometimes only the faith of Jesus himself. Without faith little happens, that is still my experience, but it is not always the patient who requires faith. So I want to describe five ways of healing in which I have been involved: but before I launch into what may seem to be spiritual realms, I would like to state very clearly that there are some very ordinary, specific, mundane things that can be done by everyone who has an interest in caring for others, in bringing healing to others and to themselves. Sleep, laughter, sport, intimacy, eating habits, hygiene, art, nature, even work, all have therapeutic qualities; all have a capacity to renew our lives. Furthermore, if we are serious about wholesomeness, then we must know that most people in the world do not die of sophisticated ailments but of malnutrition and starvation. Provision of clean water, good sanitation, fair trade, a loaf of bread, will, in fact, save more lives than all our medicines and all our prayers. 'Bread for my neighbour is a spiritual question'. The following are some of the areas of healing in which I have been involved.

The pain of guilt and sin

The first has to do with guilt and sin. I understand sin as whatever separates us from authentic living or, in conventional language, whatever keeps us apart from God. The Church's teaching has always been that Jesus Christ, the Son of God, overcomes sin and reunites us with God as our Father. His gospel is one of forgiveness: the good news is that there is a way forward in dealing with our mistakes and our problems. Sometimes I think that ministers are better at making people feel guilty than they are at making people feel forgiven. If sin is like a dark cloud over us, then Christ is the light dispelling it. If sin is like a ball and chain, then Christ is the liberator of captives. If sin is like a huge wall between us and God, or between us and one another, then Christ is the one who breaks barriers down, opens doors, reconciles people, brings pardon and peace. The reality is that many people are ill, physically, emotionally and spiritually, because the Church fails to convey that message of forgiveness, of God's love.

I was once visited by a woman whom I hardly knew. For 2 years she had been an outpatient at the local psychiatric hospital for an alcohol addiction and had previously spent 6 weeks as an inpatient. She knew that she was not cured and turned up on my doorstep in a state of great distress. When she calmed down and we were able to talk, she told me of her history, her family situation and her fears. She could see her life disintegrating before her. Eventually I said: "Well, I'm not a doctor, a psychiatrist or counsellor, but I can offer to pray with you. Do you want me to?" She said "Yes". Then something flashed through my mind and I said: "But before we pray, is there anything else you think I should know?" She blinked and said "Yes, there is something I've never been able to talk about. Before I was married I had a baby". She was concerned that he — now about 20 years — would turn up on her doorstep and embarrass the family. But mostly she felt guilty about giving him away, and shame about the whole episode. We talked a little more, and I prayed with her. I think that I may have met her a couple more times, but I met her husband a few weeks later and he almost burst into tears: "I don't know what you've done, but my wife has never been so well". If people could live free from the burdens of their past, then they would be better in every sense.

Healing past hurts and painful memories

The second kind of healing is similar. We can understand that if we have done something wrong in the past, then the way to be free of it is to own and face up to it. But what if someone has done something wrong to us? We are not responsible, so we cannot confess it and clear it up; but the memory lingers on and my experience is that the incident can have the same effect on our lives as if we had committed the fault. I refer to the healing of memories, or inner healing. The kind of things that can have serious consequences are trauma, accident, illness, bereavement, abuse in childhood or hurtful words. In such situations, I would spend time talking with the person trying to identify the painful memories: then we would relive them in prayer and, somehow, the pain of the episode is relieved. The person does not forget the incident but it no longer troubles him/her. The difficult part for the sufferer is that, eventually, they have to find the grace to forgive whoever wronged them and then they can be totally free.

I have a friend who used to be a lay preacher. He would supply pulpits when ministers were on holiday. He came to me one evening to say: "I'm going to have to give up taking services. Don't laugh. Some of the pulpits in this part of the world are quite high and I've started having attacks of vertigo, and I freeze, the service stops and I can't go on".

So we talked, and I asked him if he could remember any time in his life when he got a real scare from heights. Immediately he recalled an occasion when he and his brother were playing on the cliffs at Banff and they got stuck half way down. His brother scrambled to safety and raised the alarm but my friend was left alone for several hours watching the tide crash on the rocks below before help came.

We relived that memory in prayer and he has never been troubled since.

The laying on of hands

The third example is what most people would associate with a healing ministry; that is prayer and the laying on of hands. Here I believe that we can be used as a channel of God's Holy Spirit to bring help, healing, comfort or blessing to someone. It is what I would do if the complaint appears primarily physical. I would not normally touch the person, but just place my hand over the person's head, or near the site of the pain. It is important to stress that not everybody is healed, or at least not in the way in which they hoped. It is certainly not always immediate but I would affirm that always something is conveyed. This is not unlike the aim of doctors and nurses — sometimes to cure, often to relieve suffering, always to comfort. Perhaps the person finds peace of mind or the reassurance that someone cares; perhaps there is relief from pain, even temporarily; sometimes they can get a night's sleep or the family finds that they can cope better; sometimes death can be faced with equanimity; and sometimes people are healed.

Perhaps I should also say that I believe that the Church has a real ministry to offer around the time of death. The Catholic tradition handles this better than the Reformed Church and, while not treating the event of death with any lightness, I would say that death can be regarded as our final healing. For we are brought in faith to a place where our lives are made complete, free from sorrow and pain and, in the beautiful words of Revelation used in funeral services: 'When God shall wipe away all tears from our eyes'.

There is no doubt that the hospice movement has not only restored nursing to its rightful place in seeing all people as human beings, offering care, material and spiritual to the very end, but it has also made us re-evaluate death and our willingness to talk about it, and to face up to the final reality of life.

Confronting the power of evil

The fourth kind of healing in which I have been involved, has to do with evil. For a long time I had no understanding of the reality of evil, or of spiritual forces harmful to us. The devil was a medieval concept and evil was merely the necessary shadow side of good. I now think otherwise; in short, that we can be troubled by spiritual entities.

Some boys turned up on my doorstep when I was not at home. My wife asked them if she could help and they told her that they had been truanting school. Someone had given them an Ouija board which they had started playing with in one of their houses and things had gone wrong. She invited them to return that evening.

An Ouija board is simply a board with all the letters of the alphabet on it. A glass is upturned, people put one finger on the glass and ask the spirit of the glass questions. The glass moves from letter to letter, spelling out answers. The boys had done this, and indeed had succeeded in contacting spirits, but now they were terrified. One of them had tried to strangle his friend, another was hearing 'clip clop' sounds in his house, another had gone physically as cold as stone. When they had finished telling me their tale, I said that I was glad that they had looked to the Church, because I believe that only the Church can provide the remedy for this. I asked if they would let me pray with them and they were only too eager. So I read to them one or two stories of how Jesus dealt with such phenomena, then we prayed and they were free again. I suppose in terms of the Lord's Prayer, the first kind of healing comes when we say 'forgive us debts' (or trespasses), the second when we say 'as we forgive those who have wronged us' and the third when we pray 'but deliver us from evil'.

Healing the family tree

The last area I want to mention is called 'healing the family tree'. It is an area of therapy pioneered by Dr Kenneth McAll, a consultant psychiatrist. It is based on the belief that we have souls, that not all souls rest in peace, and that if in past generations in our family there have been suicides, occult practices, violent or unnatural deaths, abortions or miscarriages, then it is as though the soul of that person remains earthbound and interferes with the living. While Dr McAll advocates the celebration of the Eucharist for the souls of the departed, I have found simple prayer effective — in a way not unlike the kind of prayer that I would make at a funeral service, committing in love the soul to God.

Here I offer a personal experience. We have four sons, with ages ranging from 10–18 years. When our youngest was only months old, my wife noticed that he was showing very little affection; there was no closeness, no natural bonding and she began to worry that she might be in some way to blame. She considered the possibility of a subconscious disappointment that after three sons this was not a girl. The joy of having a healthy child and the experience of mothering three children did nothing to diminish the constant distancing of the child from his mother. About this time I read McAll's book *Healing the Family Tree* (1982), and we suddenly realised that between our third and fourth child, my wife had been hospitalised with a miscarriage. So we prayed, naming the unborn child, thus committing him to God. The following morning there was an immediate bonding of mother with child, a loving closeness.

Now that may have been a happy coincidence for us, but within weeks I found myself in almost exactly the same situation in my parish, except that the child was 5 years old and causing all kinds of problems at school, to the extent that the janitor had to remain within 2m of this child everywhere he went. The head teacher had called in the police, social workers and educational psychologists, all within the first term. We prayed with that family and, within days, there was a noticeable transformation in his behaviour. The boy has continued through the school with no more trouble than any other healthy child.

Conclusion

These accounts have been offered because I have come to believe that in our caring for others, we have to take spiritual realities into consideration. We all recognise that the material, tangible, visible world does not explain everything. If we are open to the possibility of exploring the spiritual, then we find, as Hamlet declared, that there are more things in heaven and earth than we dreamed of. In conclusion, I believe that it is very hard to go on caring for others unless we have an adequate sense of being cared for ourselves. We must learn how to protect ourselves from being sucked dry, learn how to draw on the spiritual, the non-material resources available to us, so that we are sufficiently replenished with what it takes to go on caring and loving. It is also vital that we see the person for whom we are caring in their totality — body, mind, spirit and social environment. There must be an equality in the relationship, no conditions or resentments, without imposition or inconsistency, so that we can indeed care for one another to our mutual benefit. For I believe in the end that it is in this exploration of how to go on caring for one another, that we discover the secret of living.

References

McAll K (1982) *Healing The Family Tree*. Sheldon Press, London

Merton T (1973) *Contemplative Prayer*. Darton, Longman & Todd, London

Temple W (1938) *Nature, Man and God*. S C M, London

Chapter 4

Ethics and the spirituality of caring

A Brian Devlin

Ethical behaviour, I believe, is the manifestation of the spirituality in caring, but little or no attention is paid to ethics in the educational preparation of professional carers. This has much to do with our failure to adequately address the major issues in health care currently confronting society. The following contribution to the debate on the spiritual dimension in caring presents a challenge to traditional views on this matter and stems from my background as a former priest in the Roman Catholic Church and from my role in harm reduction as a health promotion officer.

The essence of spirituality

Spirituality is not synonymous with prayer, meditation, contemplation, worship or mantra; and the ability to care is not dependent upon a belief in God. I suggest that the essence of the spirituality of caring is that which makes us more fully ourselves, more fully human. Some people suggest that this progression towards a fuller humanity is, in fact, a progression to sanctity, or divinity. However it is expressed, spirituality is concerned with life as lived; even the Christian tradition recognises that Jesus — God — was fully human. It is when we find our humanity that we find our divinity: and our humanity is found in ethical behaviour developed through living and interacting in community with our fellows.

Ethics and spirituality suggest two things to me: first, that the human person is capable of transcendence — of going beyond him/herself; secondly, the reason for that transcendence is that the journey itself, as well as the ultimate goal of the journey, is one wherein we find ourselves, and we define ourselves. Some people will call this journey religion. Others will not. The distinction is not important. What is important is what we do, and how we are along the journey. It is important for carers to be clear about the ethics of their apparently caring actions. A brief exploration of the following three propositions will illustrate this point:

● It can be morally justifiable to do harm in order to eventually do good
● In caring, we must distinguish between people's wants and their needs
● The choice that carers make 'to care' often involves a movement in the concept of carer to that of career. How can the career carer reconcile the two concepts?

Doing harm in order to do good

On the face of it, such a notion appears repugnant to many of us who are in the business of caring. To do harm in order that good will eventually result appears, not only a very selfish concept, but also a concept which has overtones of fascism and high-scale corruption. The concept, however, has been part of our Christian tradition for centuries. It was St Thomas Aquinas who developed the theme of doing harm in order that a greater good would prevail when he outlined the 'ethics' of self-defence. If you are being attacked by an unjust aggressor, then it is fully acceptable for you to take the means to defend yourself. However, Aquinas did suggest one caveat to this self-defence issue: the means that you use to defend yourself must be in proportion to the risk that you are in. In other words, if your attacker wants to steal your Access card, it may be disproportionate to blast his head off with the Kalashnikov rifle that you have under your jacket.

It is this issue of 'proportionality' which lies at the heart of many of the most modern debates on ethics. It is recognised that one can 'do a bad thing', for example cause pain to another person, as long as the good which is achieved outweighs the evil which is caused. It is possible for a man to act morally and cause you pain by sticking a knife into your heart, if the purpose of that action was to remove a piece of diseased tissue. However, if a man stuck a knife into your heart because your behaviour or appearance was in some way objectionable to him, then that would be less acceptable ethically!

If I am studying for an examination and have a headache, I can do two things: I can take two headache pills, and live with the fact that this drug may possibly produce some reaction in me; or I can chop my head off. Both actions have the same effect — both cure my headache. One is proportionate to the eventual end of me sitting my examination, the other is not. Likewise, if I give my last £1 coin to the beggar on the street who says "I've got three kids, a sick wife and no home", this 'good' act also has a negative effect, for it means that I have no money to give the next beggar who has '13 children, is a widower and is 2 years in arrears with his council tax'.

As carers, it is important that we should keep in mind the potential for both good and harm in our actions. What may appear to be an act entirely done through charitable reckoning, ethically speaking, will have a bad as well as a good consequence. This fact in itself does not mean that the act becomes immoral; merely that there should be a clear calculation of whether or not there is proportion between the good and evil components of the act.

Some values may be considered to be so fundamental as to be absolute. The value of life itself may be such an example. The whole ethos of our health-care system is to pay service to the value of life. Increasingly, however, we recognise that something more important than living is considered by professional carers in their care provision. Not only is the question asked, 'Can patient X live through this'?, but also 'What sort of life can he expect?' Can we not say then that euthanasia, in this sense, is already part of our health-care system? We know that in the clinical judgement of therapeutic treatment the determining factor is often not whether Mr X will eventually survive, but, rather, how can we help him now, and in the next few hours, or days or weeks to live without pain, knowing that our very palliative treatment may even hasten his death? What is the judgement that is made? Is there proportion between prescribing a death-hastening drug to a patient for whom death is imminent and one for whom death is a mere possibility? Of course we treat Mr X much differently with our pain control knowing that he has terminal lung cancer than if he has an ingrowing toenail.

The next question we must ask is, 'Why, if it is ethically acceptable (and some would argue that it is) to hasten Mr X's death through pain control, can we not prescribe for Mr X in such a way as to directly bring about his death?' Is it not contradictory that carers, those with the best interest of the other at their hearts, and indeed the patient him/herself, cannot make that decision in the light of the facts and the realities of the case, the proportion between the harm caused on the one hand (the death of Mr X and the sadness that brings) and the right of Mr X to die with dignity? The ethics of caring apparently rely on a mechanistic appraisal of how an action is carried out, as opposed to a qualitative awareness of the value of human life in relation to all of the other values that we consider.

My own area of academic interest lies in the ethics of Roman Catholicism. The Roman Catholic tradition recognises that certain acts are intrinsically evil; that certain acts, by and of themselves, carry a moral charge that always renders them negative. For example, in the official teaching of the Roman Catholic Church, all sexual acts must enhance the love between two married people, and, at the same time, they must be open to the possibility of procreation. Any act which does not hold this duality of purpose is morally unacceptable. The consequences of this approach are often bizarre. For example, masturbation in Roman Catholic teaching is intrinsically immoral. That is to say, it is always wrong regardless of circumstances. This makes the act unacceptable even if it is a means of collecting sperm for fertility analysis.

An approach to ethics which relies on some written or unwritten code, wherein certain actions in and of themselves are morally charged, is one which will result in highly dubious consequences. The Christian tradition can, therefore, cause an incomprehensible amount of spiritual suffering for individuals and communities when they fail to comply with the moral code of the Church. When we speak about ethics and the ethics of care, as carers we must reflect on what we are bringing to the caring dynamic: is it the rigour of mathematical certainty, or values that are growth producing?

Human growth is about developing new horizons collectively with our fellows as we journey through life. A system of rigid and minutely descriptive codes of ethical human behaviour will never lead us to growth. Ethical caring means finding the answers from within ourselves as individuals and in relationships with others.

Wants and needs

The spirituality of caring is the full interaction of human persons in their environment, through mature reflection and behaviour and having regard for historical and cultural sensitivities. The real spirituality of humanity is to be found in the living of life, as opposed to the purely physical phenomenon of life. In considering this dynamic of caring relative to the allocation of health-care resources, we need to distinguish between wants and needs.

The acquired immunodeficiency syndrome (AIDS) crisis has taught us much about distinguishing between needs and wants in society, and caused us to re-examine the moral foundations that underpin such distinctions. We may want to live in a world where people will not offend our own moral values; we may want to live in a world where we hark back to the old days when we were young — when black was black and white was white, the summers were long and hot, there were no beggars on the street, everyone had a job and we were proud to be British! We may want all that but our needs are different. The AIDS epidemic teaches us that. Ethically, we must address the needs of our times. Parents are burying their children; grandparents are holding the hands of their dying grandchildren and the faces that once looked up to them as young children are now the faces of those who know life and prepare for death. We may want to have someone to blame for this situation. We may want to blame the homosexual; the drug user; the prostitute. We may want to say that they are the guilty victims of this epidemic and the little babies, the haemophiliacs and the heterosexual partners are the innocents. But that is naive. The reality is that some of our children take drugs; our husbands and our wives may have sex with other people; that one day our son Adam may introduce us to his partner Steve and not Eve. In a world where love and the very act of loving itself is dangerous, we must address the needs of the community in this wartime situation of AIDS. Giving condoms to our young people, if that is our sole response to the sexual spread of human imunodeficiency virus (HIV) infection, is inadequate and minimalist. We need to do that, but we also need to teach them about love and sex in ways that are better than those currently available in our society today. We have to understand that some of our children will be gay. However difficult that may be, it is necessary to face the fact that loving our children means loving them completely; and that includes the sexuality however that is expressed. Holding to rigid, minimalist, moral codes is a recipe for unnecessary pain and suffering.

My thesis has been that spirituality is intrinsically tied to the search for human experience and human growth. The AIDS epidemic has sharply contrasted the real and the ideal world. It has taught us that what we want to believe and the situations that confront us are often at odds. As a society, as individuals, as carers and as cared for, we are ill-prepared for the challenges of modern living; ill-prepared to challenge or re-construct the political ideologies that determine how we live and how our world will be shaped. Consequently, we have no arguments for those who hold that resources are finite and care must be rationed. If we are uncertain about the moral foundations of our society, how are we to make and live with decisions not to resuscitate, to switch off life-support machines, to offer a liver transplant to patient A and not to patient B; or to move support from service X to service Y?

Career carers

Caring takes place on different levels within our society — from neighbours chatting while hanging out the washing, to social work intervention in child care. The career carer has an immense network of statutory responsibilities and regulations which define the type of care that she/he can give or is allowed to give. For some, these guidelines and rules are intensely frustrating, while for others they are a necessary and welcome protection from becoming dangerously over-involved. More importantly, however, career carers are influenced by their own value baggage, and this can have a devastating effect on their ability to provide professional caring services.

In my sessions with student nurses, I go through what I call a personal baggage questionnaire. I ask them 10 questions of an ethical or political nature. The only rules are that they have 3 seconds to answer and they must answer either 'yes' or 'no', not 'I don't know'. Generally the questionnaire starts with relatively innocuous questions such as, 'Are women better drivers than men?' 'Should Scotland be independent from the rest of the UK?' The exercise rapidly moves on to ask 'Is the embryo fully human from the moment of conception?' 'Is euthanasia ever morally justifiable?' 'Should people with AIDS be assured of absolute confidentiality?' 'Is abortion ever morally justifiable?' and usually ends with a relatively 'safe' question such as, 'Is Madonna a good role model for the under-fives of our community?' This crude exercise is really an attempt to encourage the student to consider where our values come from and also whether or not we all have values. In a class of 20 students, there will be very mixed views on many of the major issues of our time, such as abortion, euthanasia and confidentiality. The exercise helps to uncover divergent views of these aspects of care and to encourage debate on how these divergent views can affect, for example, teamwork and harmony within a clinical area.

Through the personal baggage questionnaire, we are able to see that we each of us as carers carry our baggage. This baggage comes from our family background, the newspapers we read, the views of our friends, the influences of our teachers, our culture and so on.

It is imperative that career carers are aware of their own personal baggage and how it may influence care provision. Not only do we need to be aware of the individual values that we hold, but also the corporate or the institutionalised ones that we adhere to and which give out messages to the people we serve. It is, of course, impossible to shed the baggage, but it is of great importance that we recognise it for what it is. We and the people we care for have a right to expect that we will review our attitudes to homosexuality, to drug use and to religious differences. Caring demands unconditional love. When those who are marginalised, victimised and hurt go to the carer and meet with prejudice or religious condemnation, then the nature and value of career caring has to be seriously questioned.

Conclusion

I have suggested that the spirituality in caring and the ethics of caring are synonymous and concerned with our journey to human fulfilment and maturity. Most of us reach our spiritual selves through deep and difficult personal struggle that is often made more painful by the imposition of dangerously misguided religious and political dictat. The spiritual dimension, the inner life, can be strengthened only if we acknowledge it and name it. For some it is God, for others it is the human spirit or soul. Ignoring the spiritual dimension of life leads to personal and collective dis-ease. Professional carers have a responsibility to both acknowledge the spiritual dimension of life and help nurture the individual spirit through their own ethical behaviour. This search is transforming and healing for both the carer and the cared for. The search for spirit leads to love and a better world for all.

Chapter 5

Does science need religion?

Ann Bradshaw

In May 1995, Edinburgh hit the national headlines. The furore was created when the Bishop of Edinburgh, apparently quoted out of context, or in his words 'stitched up', was said to suggest that human beings could not help being adulterous. It was all in their genes. This comment made the headlines in several newspapers. The Church Times (1995) headline read 'Bishop succumbs to genetic impulse to talk'. The whole issue seems to have arisen because the Bishop wanted religion to be informed by genetic and anthropological research. He believes that religion needs science to help us in understanding ourselves.

But, conversely, the very scientist whose whole life is based on understanding the nature of genes, the Oxford scientist, Richard Dawkins (1995), argues emphatically that science has absolutely no need for religion. He suggests that Charles Darwin lost his faith with the help of a wasp. This particular breed of female wasp lays her eggs in a caterpillar, paralysing its central nervous system but not killing it, in order to keep it alive so that the wasp grubs have fresh meat to feed on. The caterpillar, though unable to move, is still able to feel that it is being eaten alive. For Darwin this raised the question: 'How could an omnipotent and beneficent God create this kind of insect?' Darwin lost his faith but kept it hidden from his devout wife. Dawkins has no such qualms. For him there is no

God, no good and no evil; neither cruelty nor kindness. Things are merely indifferent to all suffering. There is no ultimate purpose to human life.

But the very arguments suggested by Dawkins are turned upside down by modern-day philosophers who believe that the real meaning of our lives is our own personal truth, the fruit of our existential experience. It is not surprising that there should be a distrust of science as dehumanising and impersonal, mechanical, hard and cold. And certainly among nursing writers today, it is easy to trace a distrust with Western science and what is called the 'biomedical model'. Numerous papers and books are written by nurses about the importance of repersonalising patient care with the help of personal therapies, phenomenological research and narratives of reflective practice. Indeed, we need only look at the latest nursing and midwifery publications catalogue from Churchill Livingstone as an example of what kind of books they think nurses want to buy; there are two pages of advertisements for anatomy, physiology, bacteriology and microbiology texts for nurses, but five pages for complementary therapies, or what we might call the touchy-feely approach.

Perhaps both perspectives are correct. We need science to understand our world, how we function as human beings, but we also need compassion, a moral sense of right and wrong, and a purpose in order to make sense of our lives. Nowhere can this be more true than in nursing. This chapter argues that not only is a religious viewpoint justified in the modern world but also that it is absolutely needed to justify science. It also argues that science needs to be justified. We need to recognise, the vital importance of science, not only to the world generally, but also, and particularly, to those in the nursing profession. I will start by looking at the histories of science and religion, and then how religion validates the claims of scientific rationalism, how it humanises science through compassion, and, finally, how religion provides science with a moral context, the basis for the art and science of nursing care. To clarify, I am specifying monotheistic Judaeo-Christian religion that has undergirded the development of Western medicine.

The history of scientific development and the influence of religion

In a recent article published in the newly founded *International History of Nursing Journal*, the nursing historian Anne-Marie Rafferty (1995), has argued that the reform of nursing that took place in the nineteenth century was precipitated by an unlikely alliance of religious reformers and medical doctors, or what she terms 'the brotherhood of science'. She believes that they combined in order to caricature the kind of working woman portrayed by Charles Dickens (1994) in *Martin Chuzzlewit*, Sarah Gamp. Sarah Gamp, you may remember, was described by Dickens because she represented a common figure in early Victorian England. She was a domiciliary nurse who worked in the client's home, but she was lazy and dissolute and cared nothing for the patient.

Rafferty argues that Dickens' caricature served a two-fold purpose: first, the religious idealists and philanthropists sought a moral reform, a Christianising mission of the poor; and secondly, the medical men wanted to neutralise the domiciliary nurse's female independence and power, as well as her social identification with the working class culture. Both religious reformers and medical men saw such women as Sarah Gamp as 'quacks'. Medical practitioners appealed to the Enlightenment values of rational science to disparage what they saw as superstition underlying the practice of irregular medical remedies, while nurse reformers, inspired by religious motivations, sought to denigrate the moral indiscipline and laxness of the old-style domiciliary nurse.

We might want to question Rafferty on the accuracy of her analysis; whether she is interpreting history through twentieth-century spectacles. We might also want to question her conclusions, that the Sarah Gamp style of nurse is not as bad as she is painted and actually provides a role model of nursing autonomy that we are moving towards today. We will come back to these considerations later in the chapter. Suffice to say for the present that Rafferty has demonstrated an historical truth, that in the nineteenth century science and religion were vital determinants in reforming health care. If we look more deeply into the history of science, we see the powerful influence of the Judaeo-Christian religion, both positively and negatively, on the development of science.

In his book *Science and Religion*, John Hedley Brooke (1991) argues that in the past religious beliefs served as a presupposition for the scientific enterprise because they have underwritten the uniformity of cause and effect. The development of science was the search for order in a universe regulated by an intelligent Creator. In the seventeenth century, Renè Descartes believed that he was discovering 'laws that God had put into nature', and Isaac Newton declared that the regulation of the solar system presupposed the 'counsel and dominion of an intelligent and powerful Being' (Brooke, 1991:19). Not only did the order of the universe presuppose a Divine mind, but so did the human ability to discover that order. The capacity of the human mind presupposed origins in a Divine mind. As the late sixteenth- early seventeenth-century astronomer, Johannes Kepler wrote, exposing the geometry of creation was thinking God's thoughts after him.

Religion also sanctioned science. God had revealed himself in both scripture and nature. Francis Bacon, for example, at about the same period as Kepler, pointed to the book of Daniel, chapter 12, verse 4 to argue that science was sanctioned by God himself. Knowledge was for the service of mankind. Thomas Spratt in 1667 argued that the study of science engendered piety, perseverance and humility, or Christian virtue. Religious beliefs also gave science a motive. In Holland and England in the seventeenth century, the Protestant emphasis on improving the world under the aegis of providence conferred a dignity on science as promising the glory of God and the relief of human suffering.

Among historians, there is considered to be a conflict between science and religion; between what is though to be the two contending powers. Brooke argues that this battle was not so much between science and religion but between science and dogmatic theology. He believes that such historians are looking for polarities and ignore the complementary nature of science and religion. Indeed, as Brooke sees it, the conflicts were much more likely to be between old-established science and new science. He argues that the conventional view of the conflict engaged by the Copernican revolution is not correct. It is wrong to imagine that opposition to the theory derived only from religious prejudice. Galileo seemed to have felt that his difficulties with the Catholic Church had their origins in the resentment of academic authorities who put pressure on Church authorities to denounce him. As Brooke argues, science and religion should be seen as complex social activities involving different expressions of human concern, the same individuals often participating in both.

If we turn to Sir Keith Thomas' *Religion and the Decline of Magic* (1973), we see in detail the relationship between the growth of science and the decline of magic. The sixteenth and seventeenth centuries in England are comparable with the so-called 'underdeveloped' areas of today. In the seventeenth century, doctors were unable to cure many of the frequent and common maladies. They were totally ignorant of what was going on inside the body. Internal medicine had to wait until the slow development of anatomy and physiology. Surgeons were regarded as having inferior skills compared with physicians and, without anaesthesia, people were terrified of going to them. The plague, for example, was not associated with rats but attributed to noxious vapours in the air and corrupt humours in the body. All sorts of amulets and preservatives were recommended, such as tobacco, arsenic, quicksilver and dried toads. Apothecaries outnumbered physicians five to one, so the supply of physicians was limited.

Even so, most of the poor were not affected by organised medicine. They went outside licensed practice and consulted the herbalist, so-called 'wise women', or 'great multitude of ignorant persons' as they were denounced by parliament in 1512 (Thomas, 1973:14). And it was only the poor who would consider going into either of the two London hospitals, St Thomas' or St Bartholemew's, at the end of the seventeenth century; even then one was liable to contract a fatal infection.

According to Thomas, the impact of the Protestant Reformation was to take out the magical elements of religion, the idea of objects and rituals becoming endowed with supernatural qualities and, above all, it diminished the institutional role of the Church as a

dispenser of Divine Grace. The individual was in direct relationship with God. Yet, as Bishop Latimer, a reformer, wrote in 1552:
> *'...when we be in trouble or sickness, or lose anything, we run hither and thither to witches or sorcerers whome we call wise men ...seeking aid and comfort at their hands'.*

(Thomas, 1973: 209)

One hundred years later, a Puritan, Anthony Burgess, used almost exactly the same words. Much of the magical healing reflected the old belief in the curative power of the medieval Church. It was deep-seated and ingrained. As the future Bishop of Lincoln wrote in 1621 about 'charmers, fortune tellers and wizards', it was:
> *'...scarce credible how generally and miserably our common ignorants are besotted with the opinion of their skill; and how pitifully they are gulled by their damnable impostures, through their own foolish credulity'.*

(Thomas, 1973: 291)

Thomas argues that the Church was vehemently against such practitioners of the superstitious. Nevertheless, magic and religion in the years after the Reformation were not opposed and incompatible systems. Magical elements survived in religion, and religious facets survived in magic; but the Reformation had initiated a new direction. People were taught that difficulties could only be solved by self-help and prayer to God, and even though the ordinary people continued to turn to magical remedies, astrology, charmers and soothsayers, the clergy continually warned against what they perceived to be deception. Their use continued because that was all there was. Yet magic declined even before the advent of new technology. This was partly due to the intellectual changes of the Enlightenment. Men began to believe in the ability of reason to understand, and thus have some control over nature. As Thomas argues, men became more prepared to combine impotence in the face of current misfortune with the faith that a technical solution would one day be found. A religious belief in order was the presupposition on which the work of natural science was built. Even so, Thomas concludes that if magic is to be understood as the use of 'ineffective techniques to allay anxiety when effective ones are not available, then we must recognise that no society will ever be free from it' (Thomas, 1973: 800).

If religion provided the groundwork for scientific development, then it also provided the basis for compassionate care. The Nightingale tradition revived a religious ethic just as Cicely Saunders, the founder of the modern hospice movement, was to do a century later. Their inspiration was the biblical injunctions: 'I was sick and you visited me'. 'Inasmuch as you did it for the least of these, you did it unto me'. It was the living out of the ethic of the Good Samaritan. What Nightingale did, which was the same as Cicely Saunders did with palliative care, was to bring together science and art; technical, medical and scientific knowledge, as it stood at the time, and compassion and care derived from a religious ethic. As Nightingale used doctors to teach nurses in the 1870s, so Cicely Saunders became a doctor in order to bring advances in pain relief and symptom control to the terminally ill in the 1970s. And here we might look back to Sarah Gamp, for Dickens' portrayal of her and her ilk revealed two major criticisms: first, she brought not the scientific knowledge of the day but a kind of 'folk' healing approach to patients — homemade, handed-down, anecdotal remedies; and secondly, that she did not really 'care' about her patients. She did not bring love and compassion, but a rather heartless, paid, contracted tolerance.

So much for the past, let us now turn to the need of science for religion in our health-care in today's world.

Scientific truth is justified by religion

As the philosopher, Professor Roger Trigg (1993) argues, religion played a major part historically, in providing the intellectual climate by which modern science flourished. He believes that religion has the same relevance for science in today's world. God is the source of reason and the ultimate explanation for an inherent rational structure in the world. But, as we have seen with Richard Dawkins, this kind of explanation is not accepted by everyone. Rather than accepting the limits of science in explaining reality, some scientists have argued that the only legitimate truth to be discovered is scientific truth. This was the view of a group of philosophers in the 1920s and 1930s, the Vienna Circle, who argued that knowledge is derivable from experience, and the task of philosophy was that of logic to help create a unified science. What is beyond the reach of human beings, ideas of God, for example, can safely be dismissed, or as the philosopher Wittgenstein said, 'what we cannot speak about we must consign to silence' (Trigg, 1993:23).

Trigg argues that this kind of thinking opened the way for the rational and realist basis and foundations for science to be cut away. For, as Wittgenstein came to believe, truth no longer exists 'out there', abstracted from the world we find ourselves in, our everyday experiences and situations. Instead, truth is a personal source of meaning disclosed in the different ways we live. He called this our language games. Each game has different rules understandable only in their particular context. Science is just one way of seeing the world, one particular game among many, and, as Trigg shows, the status of science as an arbiter of truth is shattered. It cannot claim rational justification or realism. The claims of science are merely one set of claims among many:

> *'We may go on being scientists because that is the way we have been educated, but faced with alternative societies preferring to put their trust in oracles, astrology or whatever, we can only indulge in name-calling'.*

(Trigg, 1993: 32)

Wittgenstein's position according to Trigg, is very similar to Thomas Kuhn's (1970) belief that scientific theories are incommensurable. Science advances not gradually and rationally but by paradigm shifts; the prevailing scientific theory is overturned by a new one. And here we might see the link with nursing, for among nursing theorists there is a great interest in Kuhn's ideas and their use to justify the argument that the Western scientific model is but one model alongside which there are other paradigms and possibilities, including those remedies and therapies, often derived from Eastern philosophies, which we now call 'complementary therapy'. This might help us to understand Rafferty's advocacy of the housewifely 'Sarah Gamp' kind of nurse, practising homely but unscientific folk medicine as a way forward for nursing. To use Wittgenstein's concept, this is an alternative language game for nursing, clearly separating and distancing what nurses do, and are, from what doctors do and are.

We may be reminded that this is not so much historical progress but a return to ideas prevalent in history. It is the idea that, in some way, magic may actually work when conventional medicine fails. Sir John Vane (1995), Nobel prize winner for medicine, argues that this return to 'quack' remedies — extracts of flowers, herbal remedies, ginseng, elixir of bees — as well as therapies such as acupuncture, homeopathy, reflexology and iridology have more in common with black magic and voodoo. In his view, they are a return to the superstitions of the Middle Ages, eye of newt and toe of frog, untried and untested.

The television doctor, Rob Buckman argues that the value of such therapies is a placebo effect and therein lies their value (Buckman and Sabbagh, 1993). But the question is also raised as to whether science is preserved. Does belief in the healing powers of magic, whether by potions or by therapies, inevitably go hand-in-hand with disbelief in, or perhaps distrust of medicine? However often proponents of complementary therapies, for example, state that they are not alternative but complementary to scientific medicine, it seems inevitable that the valuing of one leads to the devaluing of the other. Perhaps this is inevitable when these proponents derive validation for their methods from the qualitative, experiential paradigm rather than from experimental science. As it is argued, such methods cannot be verified by scientific, quantitative methods because they rely on a different, incommensurable world-view: a world-view of feeling and experience that cannot be crudely weighed and measured.

Yet, and accordingly, Trigg argues that such relativism of competing incommensurable claims is inevitable if science is taken away from its metaphysical grounding. If we are to trust science as being able to disclose the reality of the world for us, and the ability of technology and medicine to cure and prevent diseases, then we need to believe in prior created order, a realism that is not arbitrary or chaotic but is rooted in the way the world is. Science needs religion to provide a justification for its generalisability and verifiability.

Science is humanised by religion

Many of the criticisms of science have been those of 'nothing buttery'. 'Nothing buttery' is a term used to describe the view that the human being is nothing more than a set of mechanical, interacting systems. Here we need to be clear. We know that a person is composed of sets of interacting systems, but what is disputed is the claim made by scientists, such as Dawkins, that that is all he/she is. The existentialists, such as Heidegger, are prominent in this criticism of 'nothing buttery', and it underlies the work of nurses, such as Patricia Benner (1985). As such, it is a twentieth-century movement; a criticism of the overwhelming dominance of science and technology in our lives; a belief that we need to preserve the humanity of human beings. But it has also, and we can argue primarily and originally, found expression and justification because of the religious viewpoint. The wholeness of the human being, his/her unique personhood, derives from his/her createdness in the image of God.

History indisputably shows that the development of care and compassion for the sick derived from religious motivations. Lord Walton in the 1990 *Harveian Oration to the Royal College of Physicians* reminds us that it was the Christian ethic that humanised Greek medicine and extended care to people who could not be cured. This was the practice of agape or caritas, inspired and altruistic love for one's neighbour. Throughout the centuries, this primary motivation founded hospitals and nursing orders, but where the spirit attenuated or weakened, as it did with the Enlightenment of the eighteenth century, religious fervour died and became an outward shell, and the care of the sick was consequently affected. Hence the contractualism of 'Sarah Gamp' nursing.

But let us remind ourselves of Rafferty's argument; that the Sarah Gamp nurse was unfairly stereotyped because of an agenda set, not only by doctors but also by religious people. Dickens wrote his story against the background of the late eighteenth and early nineteenth-century religious revival of Methodism and Evangelicalism; of Wilberforce's fight against the slave trade, Shaftesbury's factory reforms and Elizabeth Fry's reform of prisons. So let us read how Dickens, with grim irony, describes the Sarah Gamp school of nursing — the nursing experts of his day.

'Mrs Gamp solaced herself with a pinch of snuff, and stood looking at him [the patient] with her head inclined a little sideways, as a connoisseur might gaze upon a doubtful work of art. By degrees, a horrible remembrance of one branch of her calling took possession of the woman; and stooping down, she pinned his wandering arms against his sides, to see how he would look if laid out as a dead man. While eating and drinking, she moralised. "What a blessed thing it is to make sick people happy in their beds and never mind one's self as long as one can do a service!"' Dickens is heavy with irony: 'She moralised in the same vein until her glass was empty, and then adminstered the patient's medicine, by the simple process of clutching his windpipe to make him gasp, and immediately pouring it down his throat. "I a'most forgot the piller, I declare!" said Mrs Gamp, drawing it away. "There! Now he's comfortable as he can be, I'm sure! I must try to make myself as much so as I can."' (Dickens, 1994: 376-7). With that, Sarah Gamp pulls the pillow out from under the patient's head in order to use it for her own requirements.

Later in the book, Sarah Gamp takes another patient by the collar and gives him a dozen shakes backward and forward in the chair. This, Dickens says, was an exercise considered by the members of the Sarah Gamp school of nursing '(who are very numerous among professional ladies) as exceedingly conducive to repose, and highly beneficial to the nervous functions.' Its effect in this instance was to render the patient so giddy and addle-headed, that he could say nothing more; which Mrs Gamp regarded as a triumph of her art. '"There!" she said, loosening the old man's cravat, in consequence of his being rather rather black in the face after this scientific treatment. "Now, I hope, you're easy in your mind. If you should turn at all faint, we can soon revive you, sir, I promige you. Bite a person's thumbs, or turn their fingers the wrong way," said Mrs Gamp, smiling with the consciousness of at once imparting pleasure and instruction to her auditors, "and they comes to, wonderful, Lord bless you!"'

What Dickens shows us was a situation where there was neither scientific method nor genuine compassion, and it was precisely this that nursing reform sought to change. But it was able to do this because it held the Sarah Gamp school of nursing up to an objective, religiously informed and tested measure that found it wanting. We might wonder whether, according to modern nursing thinking, we have lost that absolute measure and replaced it with a personal subjectivity that is not very different to the Sarah Gamp method. After all, as Dickens makes clear, Sarah Gamp was an autonomous, empowered and experienced nurse who spoke highly of her patients and the effectiveness of her nursing practice, and was extremely favourably reviewed by her very many nursing colleagues. Her own reflections on her practice, supported by her nursing peers, confirmed to her her great value as a nurse. Indeed, her touch was therapeutic for her patients. Would she thus conform to Patricia Benner's concept of today's nursing expert? Rafferty seems to imply that she does.

Science is given a moral foundation by religion

The advances in science and technology do not in themselves tell us whether and how they should be used. We can abort damaged or unwanted babies; we can end life painlessly for the terminally ill; we can create life in test tubes for infertile women; we can prolong the lives of brain-dead people; but, should we? Science itself cannot answer this question. We need some kind of answer and this is from the realms of ethics. What guides our lives? As the Cambridge theologian, Janet Martin Soskice (1994: 22) writes:

'One doctor said, "I can't tell you exactly when a patient has died: I can tell you when her heart stops beating, or when she stops breathing independently, or when there is no pulse or brain

*activity, but to say exactly when she had died — that's no longer a
medical judgment". The scientific contribution was, one could
say, morally neutral.'*

Here Martin Soskice argues, the religious viewpoint is vital, for only
this can uphold the value, indeed the sanctity, of the human being,
created in the image of God. And Martin Soskice cites the
arguments of Helga Kuhse and Peter Singer, who blame centuries
of the Christian religion for curtailing human freedoms. The
freedom that they are arguing for is that of infanticide, the ending
of life of severely sick and disabled babies. This is, after all, not much
different to abortions offered to parents of handicapped foetuses.

Indeed, a moving article by Dominic Lawson (1995), editor of
The Spectator, written 2 weeks after the birth of his daughter with
Down's syndrome, likens abortion to a form of infanticide. He
describes his profound shock at the attitudes of acquaintances who
wondered why his wife had not had the Down's syndrome test that
would have enabled her to abort the handicapped baby. For
Lawson, an atheist, such thoughts are unthinkable. But perhaps he
should have realised how this kind of thinking is inevitable in a
modern, secular world. For, as Martin Soskice concludes, without
God and without the sanctity of the person made in the image of
God, men and women will become not free and in control of their
own lives and purposes, but mere objects to manipulate in a world
of manipulable objects, as Kuhse and Singer propose.

Conclusion

I have argued that science is not only compatible with religion, but
that it needs religion. Science needs religion to justify its realist
claims; science needs religion to give it humanity; science needs
religion to make it moral. Above all, science is limited. It can tell
us about our world but not about the meaning of the world — or
the meaning and purpose of our lives.

Let us end with a quotation from the seventeenth-century
theologian and eminent scientist Blaise Pascal:

'Let man now return to himself to consider what he is, compared
with all that is; let him deem himself a stray in this out-of-the-way
corner of nature. And then, from this tiny cell in which he is
lodged — I mean the universe — let him learn to prize the earth,
kingdoms, towns, and himself, at their real value. What is man
in the Infinite?'

(Pascal, 1959: 71)

References

Benner P (1985) Quality of life: a phenomenological perspective on
explanation, prediction and understanding in nursing science. *Adv Nurs
Sci* 1(8): 1–14

Brooke JH (1991) *Science and Religion*. Cambridge University Press,
Cambridge

Buckman R, Sabbagh K (1993) *Magic or Medicine?* Macmillan, London

Church Times (1995) Bishop succumbs to genetic impulse to talk. *Church
Times* 19 May: 1

Dawkins R (1995) No mercy on the violent river of life. *Daily Telegraph*,
10 May

Dickens C (1994) *Martin Chuzzlewit*. Penguin, London

Kuhn T (1970) The Structure of Scientific Revolutions. University of
Chicago Press, Chicago

Lawson D (1995) All you need is life. *The Spectator*, 17 June: 15–16

Martin Soskice J (1994) Creation and relation. In: Fulford KWM, Gillett
G, Martin Soskice J, eds. *Medicine and Moral Reasoning*. Cambridge
University Press, Cambridge: 19–28

Pascal B (1959) *Pensées*. SCM, London

Rafferty A-M (1995) The anomoloy of autonomy: space and status in early
nursing reform. *Int Hist Nurs J* 1(1): 43–56

Thomas K (1973) *Religion and the Decline of Magic*. Penguin,
Harmondsworth

Trigg R (1993) *Rationality and Science.* Blackwell Scientific, Oxford

Vane J (1995) A triumph for the forces of ignorance. *Daily Mail* 22 June

Walton J (1990) *Harveian Oration to the Royal College of Physicians.* Royal College of Physicians, London

Epilogue

Dr E Farmer

*'The closer people in need of professional help move toward a
consideration of such spiritual issues as fear of death, loneliness
and lack of meaning in their lives, the less likely they are to find
professional workers who can be of assistance'*

(Krippner, 1995: 22)

The search for meaning in life is as old as humankind; and the roots
of dogmatism are also ancient. The papers gathered in this volume
are intended to initiate peaceful and wise debate on the spiritual
dimension in caring to replace the acrimony which so often ensues
when the subject is raised.

In the first of her contributions to this volume, Ann Bradshaw
provides an eloquent and scholarly review of nursing's ontological
and epistemological history. She believes that the spiritual
dimension is the breath of God within the human being that
transcends and cements the physical, psychological and social
dimensions of personhood and is that which makes a human being
more than the sum of his parts.

Jean Watson's paper began with a reference to the killing fields
of Bosnia and the persistent violence towards, and fear of people
who are in some way different. This reminder is important for the

debate which the publication of these papers seeks to initiate.
Michael Leunig (1990) quite simply but profoundly explains the
propensity for violent disagreement among humans in the
following way:

There are only two feelings. Love and fear.
There are only two languages. Love and fear
There are only two activities. Love and fear
There are only two motives, two procedures, two frameworks,
two results. Love and fear
Love and fear

Undoubtedly the views of Bradshaw and Watson are different, but
this should be a welcomed contribution to the evolution of the
discipline and not something to be feared. Jean Watson believes that
human beings are capable of transcending time and space through
the universal spirit or essence which transcends the self to a higher
degree of consciousness. In that sense, human beings are connected
with the impersonal life force which underpins all creation in which
matter and spirit are indistinguishable. Ann Bradshaw
acknowledges a personal, biblical, God of love. Are these views
irreconcilable? The differences are, after all, about process not
product; both subscribe to the view that love is the spiritual cement
of humanity and community.

David Lunan also focuses on love as the ultimate spiritual reality
and holds that any genuine experience of love is an authentic
experience of God. His remarkable accounts of spiritual healing
raise questions about the nature of healing. Again, is this source of
healing a personal God or an impersonal life force reached through
a higher degree of consciousness — or either of these? Brian Devlin
believes that the essence of the spirituality of caring is that which
makes us more fully ourselves; more fully human. His contribution
was concerned with right and good ways to live and he reminds us
of the suffering which results when decisions about the right and
good way to live are reduced to sets of minimalist rules. Are the
views of these authors to be considered in opposition or apposition?
This was the question that prompted Ann Bradshaw's second
contribution to this volume.

Bradshaw argues that nursing has seriously lost its focus and direction and argues for a return to the theological principles of the Judaeo-Christian approach to care as convenant, reiterated by Nightingale. A return to these roots, she argues, will rescue nurses and nursing from the morass created by the philosophical incoherence which she believes is evident in current nursing theories. All philosophical argument is concerned with showing how a particular case is linked with other things that are already accepted. Much philosophic argument is negative in kind, showing that certain assumptions lead to impossible consequences. The argument never establishes the case but merely assumes something to be true for the time being. The fact is that the foundations of positivistic science are being shaken by new theories arising from quantum physics, chaos theory and evolutionary biology. People once laughed at the notion of germ theory and space exploration. These and many more discoveries were made only because researchers moved into unconventional areas. Nurses must purposefully enter the ferment of human progress and contribute to the remodelling of the health sciences. This journey will inevitably lead us down some blind alleys — and in this regard we will share the fate of all scholars.

As Dossey (1995) has noted:

'One of the greatest impediments to progress in science is to assume that our fundamental concepts are basically complete. The never have been.'

In support of this statement Dossey offers a quotation from a paper given by Mary Hesse (a mathematician and philosopher of science at Cambridge University:

'Abandonment of the deterministic world-view in physics has made it more difficult to regard the existing state of science as finally legislative of what is and what is not possible in nature. The very fact that what appeared for three centuries to be an absolute true and universal theory has been shown to be false must cast doubt on all future claims of science to have reached such a universal theory. Science is continually growing and changing, sometimes quite radically. It is far less easy to see it

today as a monolithic and cumulative progress toward the whole
truth than was the case a hundred years ago. We are by no means
sure, even in physics, that existing quantum theories will prove
adequate in sciences other than physics, and in the sciences of
complex systems such as the human psyche and human social
groups we have only the bare beginnings of any theories at all.'

Ann Bradshaw has given a somewhat extreme warning of the fate
that waits nurses who chose to see the world through the new
scientific paradigm. Graphic descriptions of Dickens' Sarah Gamp
are used to warn against the rejection of scientific reductionism and
the inclusion of alternative therapies in the repertoire of nursing
interventions. In response to this, it is first necessary to make a
distinction between religion and spirituality. According to
Krippner (1995):

'The word "spiritual" can be used to describe aspects of human
behaviour and experience that reflect an alleged transcendent
intelligence or process. This transcendent entity inspires devotion
and directs behaviour. These spiritual aspects of behaviour and
experience are evident among human beings whenever an
awareness of a broader life meaning goes beyond the immediacy
of everyday expediency and material concerns.'

Krippner (1995) holds that:

'the word 'spiritual' is not synonymous for 'religious'; a religion is
an institutionalised body of believers who accept a common set of
beliefs, practices and rituals regarding spiritual concerns and
issues. People who have internalised these beliefs and practices are
generally spiritual. In addition, many people are spiritual
without being religious in the sense of participating in organised
religion. Conversely, a person can be religious without being
spiritual: many members of religious institutions perform the
necessary rituals and accept the creed (at least superficially),
although their ethics, morals and day-to-day practice of religion
do not match their professed beliefs.'

Science does not need religion but it is attempting to reconnect scientific endeavours with spiritual values. This reconciliation is actively resisted by religious orthodoxy and by a scientific establishment which is driven by self-interest. Many reputations have been made and much personal wealth has accrued from adherence to reductionist science. Certainly, the science of Newton and Descartes has been most successful in guarding against self-delusion; but in separating mind, body and spirit, it has failed miserably to create health.

The autonomous practice of Sarah Gamp and that of the modern nurse are **not** comparable. The new scientific paradigm does not reject the rigorous examination of phenomena. It does, however, recognise that various forms of knowledge are used by people in their everyday lives. We have yet to understand how these forms of knowledge are meaningful in individual lives. This point was well recognised by the World Health Organization (Mahler, 1977) which, in 1977, adopted a resolution urging governments to encourage the use of traditional, holistic approaches to healing. In this regard, the interrelationship of the environmental, ecological and social systems was clearly acknowledged. It is worth noting that the church is full of non-rational rituals that nevertheless have meaning in the spiritual life. They are rituals of connection, love and transformation.

What we now call 'alternative therapies' **must** be subjected to rigorous testing but the methods we use to test these will be different because of the philosophical origins of the therapies to which Ann Bradshaw urges us to pay attention. To do this, we have to set aside preconceived biases. One of these concerns the absolute value of the controlled, double-blind, clinical trial. As Ken Wilbur (1995) noted in response to a criticism of its general use:

'I always found it odd — hilarious, actually — that the double-blind is a self-contradictory endeavour. According to orthodox medicine, consciousness has no significant effect on physical states and yet the double-blind is set up to prevent consciousness of what is actually occurring, precisely because consciousness of the situation will profoundly alter physical

*outcomes. The double-blind assumes that which it officially
denies: consciousness is causal.'*

This is not a call to reject a valued technique — merely a plea to
recognise its limitations in a different world-view. Are alternative
forms of healing a misinterpretation of the natural world and how
it works? In a mechanistic paradigm, the answer must be 'yes'. In a
holistic world-view, not at all.

Is Ann Bradshaw's definition of the spiritual dimension as the
breath of God within the human being challenged by the new
paradigm science which increasingly equates spirituality with the
evolution of consciousness? When asked how she would define
consciousness, Candace Pert (a neurological scientist and research
professor) replied:

*'Well, it's hooked up with God. It's ultimate knowledge and
wisdom. ...On some level, all the information in the universe is
available to all the other information in the universe, and that,
to me, is God.'*

A number of experiments on the effects of conscious intention have
demonstrated physical consequences. The study of the complex
network of relations in the matter and energy transactions of living
systems offers a fresh perspective for biology, medicine and for
nursing. New insights into the interrelationships between mind and
matter offer new possibilities for the relief of suffering.

If we are to make sensitive, ethical progress in life then we should
not be concerned with which view should prevail but with a
genuine search for shared meanings. We need to respect and
understand the different expressions of human concern. If we as
nurses do not honour all different forms of knowledge (most of
which have been known to women throughout history) then before
long we shall surely be worthy of comparison with the ignorant,
heartless, intolerant, materialistic Sarah Gamp. We have replaced
our care and compassion with the ironmongery of modern
medicine and are now in danger of being dragged blindly into an
era when the reductionism associated with genetics will present

moral dilemmas which our education has left us ill-equipped to address.

However we define the universe, or think about life and its origins, there is general agreement that it has non-rational, mysterious and unsayable qualities. The authors of the chapters contained in this small volume are agreed on the need for love, care and compassion in our world, and the exploration of these facets of life seems to be a good place to begin our journey towards shared meanings.

References

Dossey L (1995) How should alternative therapies be evaluated? An examination of fundamentals. *Alternative Therapies* 1(2): 6–10, 79–85

Horrigan B (1995) Candace Pert, PhD: Neuropeptides, AIDS and the science of mind-body healing. *Alternative Therapies* 1(3): 70–6

Krippner S (1995) A cross-cultural comparison of four healing models. *Alternatives Therapies* 1(1): 21–9

Leunig M (1990) *A Common Prayer*. Collins Dove, Victoria, Australia

Mahler H (1977) The staff of Aesculapius. *World Health* **Nov 3**

Wilber K (1995) Double-blind method assumes what it denies. Letter to the editor. *Alternative Therapies* 1(4): 12

PENGUIN BOOKS

If All the World and Love Were Young

Stephen Sexton lives in Belfast. His poems have appeared in *Granta, POETRY, The Stinging Fly* and *Poetry Ireland Review*. His pamphlet, *Oils*, was the Poetry Book Society's Winter Pamphlet Choice. He was the winner of the 2016 National Poetry Competition and the recipient of an ACES award from the Arts Council of Northern Ireland. He received an Eric Gregory Award in 2018.

STEPHEN SEXTON

If All the World and Love Were Young

PENGUIN BOOKS

PENGUIN BOOKS

UK | USA | Canada | Ireland | Australia
India | New Zealand | South Africa

Allen Lane is part of the Penguin Random House group of companies
whose addresses can be found at global.penguinrandomhouse.com

First published in Great Britain by Penguin Books 2019

002

Copyright © Stephen Sexton, 2019

The moral right of the author has been asserted

Set in 10/13.75 pt Warnock Pro
by Integra Software Services Pvt. Ltd, Pondicherry
Printed in Great Britain by Clays Ltd, Elcograf S.p.A.

A CIP catalogue record for this book is available from the British Library

ISBN: 978–0–141–99002–6

www.greenpenguin.co.uk

NOTE

In the summer of 1998, when I was nine, my mother took a photograph of me playing *Super Mario World* (1990) in the small spare room in our house. My back is to the camera. The television was positioned so it faced out from the corner of the room where the wall met the patio door. To my left, I could see the garden, along which a little river ran and, over the fields, a dense forest. To my right, there was the huge block of the television, which was already fifteen or sixteen years old. My eyes drifted between these two positions. Because of the flash of the camera and the glare of the television screen, it's impossible to tell which of the following levels I'm playing.

The Super Nintendo is a 16-bit console. Put simply, 16-bit refers to how much memory the system can process at one time.

In memory of my mother for my father for my brother

'*Photography is seen as an acute manifestation
of the individualized "I", the homeless private
self astray in an overwhelming world.*'

– Susan Sontag

*Yet I cannot escape the picture
Of my small self in that bank of flowers:
My head among the blazing phlox
Seemed a pale and gigantic fungus.*

– John Ashbery

'*It's a-me, Mario!*'

– Mario

PART ONE

Yoshi's Island

Yoshi's House

These are the days of no letters the magenta mailbox jitters
out of the visible spectrum babies chirp in our holly tree
mountains yield to the foreground and sadly again
       they're beautiful:
my friends scattered in the lowlands the fire seizes in the grate
the smoke signals across the eaves say all I really mean to say
I have gone to rescue my friends I'll think of you and you and you.

Yoshi's Island 1

Here spotted mountains and cirrus here sloping plateaux drawn
        down on
carnivorous plants and no sun gold by the cherish underground
fly agaric throbs everywhere with fire plants and dinosaurs.
In these days new as tomorrow there is joy to be recorded:
the tender steps in other lands all the flowers of the garden.
My mother winds her camera the room is spelled with
        sudden light:
a rush of photons at my back a fair wind from the spectral world.
I remember myself being remembered a little lotus
a cross-legged meditant for whom the questions floating in the air
are for a future self to voice decades from now who will return
again and again to this room and these moments of watershed.
It will be an adventure I think it will be an adventure
the future is cannon blasting yes I must have dreamt this her voice
narrows into dreams of such things ships sink at the edge of
        the world.

Yellow Switch Palace

On Kappa Mountain past the great lake circumscribed
     with goldenrod
the abandoned palace is full of treasure glowing underground
in granaries and arsenals an economy of losses
and gains the beloved is gone but there is always the story.
Should a Kappa step out of myth made of scales and razory claws
a shell of keratinous scutes the hard beak of an octopus
and a vulnerability to kicks on the top of the head
should he step wet out of the lake I will offer to him kindness.
I will offer soba noodles in soy I will offer my name
written on cucumber floated on the lake whatever the cost.

Yoshi's Island 2

Pixels and bits pixels and bits their perpendicularity:
one of the worlds I live in is as shallow as a pane of glass.
The threshold of the window sets a frame around the holly tree
wild funguses slimy with dew and toxicity the rubies
of holly berries sing on the branches the robins hide among
and the veins of ivy vines wind around the slumping trunk
      and boughs
sloe berries in the blackthorn and the carcinogenic bracken.
Groundsels loiter along the low dashed wall the daisies loll about.
One summer's day I'm summoned home to hear of cells which
      split and glitch
so haphazardly someone is called to intervene with poisons
drawn from strange and peregrine trees flourishing in
      distant kingdoms.
We take the air in the garden bitter with berries and mushrooms
too toxic to eat where the grass bows in an unexpected breeze.

Yoshi's Island 3

Today I climbed the Windy Mount the highest peak in this region.
My singular wish was to see what its elevation offered.
With one companion my brother who is no better or worse than
anyone else I saw blankets of mushroom fields reducible
to patchworks what the birds' eye view must see of farms
        in Genoa.
I went so far up the broken path I supposed I should almost
see the curve of the planet or the whim on which the waves begin
but for the first time in some time I thought of our father at home
the Sirocco in from the south turtle doves in the huge wheat fields.

Yoshi's Island 4

Salt water everywhere low tides undulate a flotsam of mines
the archipelago aswim with joyful blue-white puffer fish
and in a neighbouring province saguaro prowl a feline prowl.
The ankle-deep children's pool on the peninsula buoyed us up
aboard a heavy pedalo the likeness of a giant swan
almost unmaneuverable about the tropical island
silly with plastic palms and shale from whose hollow we called
    to land
to our mother on the seafront between the artificial pool
and the sunstruck coastal waters who beckons us back
    to harbour.
Since it's August she begins the idle effacement of dying
the many prickles of needles of many exotic compounds
hormones and corticosteroids the stiffening of the larynx
mouth the dry of the walk alone into the desert finding there
those cactuses their open arms and their long curious shadows.

#1 Iggy's Castle

My dreams reply the garden has become an ocean of lava
a precinct of spewing tephra the rock like black honey folding
over again impossibly and yet on a shaky island
someone stands surrounded by fire who says to go on
        without me.
So there is a sound in the house when I wake mice under
        the moon
my mother who cannot sleep halves a bright grapefruit whose
        feet whose toes
whose hands whose fingers whose ankles whose head she says
        are on fire.

Donut Plains

Donut Plains 1

The land of flight feathers no birds backstop Chuck chucks
    his knuckleballs
the shrubs are off the Scoville scale. The little house on the border
keeps a mantelpiece abrim with dust Delftware porcelain
    knick-knacks
sixteen ceramic cows rowboats on the lake in grey photographs.
The lie of the land is the shape of the north of Ireland likewise
missing a lump from its body where the lake fills with eels zigzagged
from the Sargasso like needles of glass light slowed
    through sodium.
The little house on the east shore of the lake has something in it.
The chimney trickles smoke the hearth interprets cords
    of sycamore.
This is not our house but its walls are flowered with our images:
us as babies pink and sleeping and as children formally posed
in green and red fleeces zipped up to the chin in any weather
in the questionable fashions of the early nineteen-nineties
in the sepia-warmed wedding pictures long before we were born
in our relatives' glowing eyes whose faces are written in light.

Donut Plains 2

Henry goes west on a ship to meet the Blue Mountains of Sydney.
Henry goes south and burns in the sun through Canberra
    to Melbourne.
The Princess of Tasmania docks and Henry sails aboard her.
Henry goes down in the mines of Tasmania for zinc and lead.
It is 1964 and collapse collapse Henry is dead.
20 or so years and she gives me her brother's name to mine with.
Down I go with bats and pyrite slow progress and
    inching landslides
canary-yellow minerals words do not contain their echoes.
Jacques says a name contains something like an abyss I
    wonder Jacques.
Somewhere underground a treasure chamber is dumb
    with emeralds:
where are you you might ask aloud where are you it might
    answer back.

Green Switch Palace

The stone cottage long abandoned by disenchanted farmers' sons
crumbles is unsalvageable its acreage dreams of limestone
yet it has in it echoes of *far other worlds and other seas*
annihilating all that's made to a green thought in a green shade.
Mosses explode within its walls: hunter shamrock harlequin mint
emerald persian paris lime chartreuse viridian midnight.

Donut Ghost House

What is there to be afraid of? Whatever moves in the rafters
a sparrow's nest in the chimney stuck with hay and pigeon feathers
a knock knock knock on the slate roof is hello yourself long ago
and hello an afterimage after all one image pressed to
and escaping through another. As the world of the living peers
out into the world of the dead as the isle is full of noises
as the draught catches the blue door as its keyhole's made
    of nothing
as the fireplace crackles and offers the light of the forest
the sparrow leaves its nest of eggs or maybe the sparrow doesn't.

Top Secret Area

I have been trying to tell you
she plants roses in the garden
she plants roses in the garden
she plants roses in the garden

she plants roses in the garden
she plants roses in the garden
she plants roses in the garden
she plants roses in the garden
she plants roses in the garden
she plants roses in the garden

the secret of infinite lives:
she pliant flows in the journal
sea plants wrasses in the ocean
she paths road signs from
   the station
sea plans ruses in the argot
seaplanes rising from the water
sea froze rolling in the harbour
see pain trilling in the garden
she planes ruins in the jargon
see plinths raising in devotion

Donut Secret 1

I only know the night birds by their lullabies which echo through
the darkened fields and countryside like shepherds
     singing anything
they can to keep themselves awake: the names of all the villages
and towns they'll visit homewardly the names their children
     might have had
the names of all the fish they know who unlike me are fast asleep:
wrasses sleep tilapia sleep the hogfish sleeps the dogfish sleeps
the catfish sleeps the salmon sleeps the tuna sleeps the
     sunfish sleeps.
And sleep do the millions of eels from the Sargasso like needles
the kelp ripples in the current and I have been holding my breath.
Anglerfish doze in the trenches luminescent esca glowing.
.Night itself sleeps sweet on my chest and she quarters a
     bright grapefruit.

Donut Secret House

The little house on the east shore of the lake has something in it.
It is night-time when I arrive a mist settles against the roof
picture windows in wooden frames return my image in their glass
the dashed grey brick worries off here and there a giant
      fruitless bush
almost a story high leans on the western wall or does the wall
whose foundations bear high water when the floods
      come annually
gales when the season supposes it lean against the giant bush?

Donut Secret 2

It is winter in the Ulster Hospital and winter outdoors
and winter in our hemisphere the tilt of the planet says so.
Since she has lost her sense of taste we have dinner
      in McDonald's.
If I'm going to die she says might as well go to McDonald's.
The kitchen bleeps and chirps and blips the cryptolect of ICU's
whose automatic song desires no singer's articulation.
Her hair is thin under the light and surgery will be discussed
tonight while fleets of gritters salt all the main arterial routes.
The country roads we travel home by purple and glisten
      with frost
underneath the constellations and the Sagittarian moon.

Donut Plains 3

The bridge is split and trussed oak trunks laid across the gorge
      the water
dapples against the edges of imagine the sheer drop the bridge
swaying in the south-western wind the white-clawed sea
      skulking below.
One thing must become another chop chop the tree becomes
      a bridge
forest becomes a labyrinth whose prospect one climbs higher for
and from the falling dream you jolt somehow having
      landed having
been nowhere but long in front of the beautiful television.

Donut Plains 4

Those blue afternoons of winter the air crisp and cool as thinking.
Kappa swarmed in every colour under a waxing crescent moon
which seemed to augur well for me once I was falling to my death
once I survived the fall landing in a trench scooped and
     jigsawed out
of the earth hello earth nice to see you amazed to be alive
where chestnuts conk and roll around and others parachute
     from trees.
During the dark century's wars I read children filled their pockets
with chestnuts to render into acetone to render into
cordite into shells sitting primed in the rifles of their cousins.
What will be the consequences of the trees waving in the wind
chestnuts in the hospital grounds the low dazzling winter sun?

#2 *Morton's Castle*

The wind blew as it blows over the ramparts and the battlements
along the merlons and crenels the fieldwork of Morton's Castle.
A wind jigs on the lake surface a dilemma sharpens its horns.
The castle is riddled with traps where boulders grin and
      bounce below
a mace that swings in rotary its fullest circle pendulum
and glassless gothic window frames in ancient hallways long
      as dreams.
In the castle is the surgeon lean and elegant as a fork.
This is how it's done precisely he says sharpening his finger
to a point so fine it's finer than any sparkle in his eye.

Vanilla Dome

Vanilla Dome 1

Now we must beware of the cave after a few days of fasting
the anesthesiologist apothecaries carefully
and the personable surgeon goes under the skin precisely.
I go down into the dark mines where my name clings like
      a horseshoe
and deeper until the stream of my blood runs as black as the coal.
In Kimberley diamonds have grown in the walls for thousands
      of years.
The mines dug out by hand have left countless thousands dead
      having not
chosen the underground if they could help it. And so
      bright diamonds
is what I think of diamonds grown without a thimbleful of light
beautiful time goes by slowly and the surgeon covers his tracks.

Vanilla Dome 2

The Big Hole was excavated 240m
deep but has since filled up with rain water and general run-off.
It's this I think of: paddling on its azure eye lazily
in some leaky rowboat Sundays from now when the whole
    thing's over
and I'll say wasn't it strange how we used to live like that?
    And she
will say do you think it's strange to miss yourself? as the sun
    goes down.

Red Switch Palace

The Big Hole was excavated when there was something there
     to want.
Spelunkers marvel at its size but overlook the Sharashka
built into the basin. It's said there are prisoners kept even
now alchemists smashing rubies into dust into medicine
as though dabbing it on the tongue might remedy hematomas
as though wearing the grains of it might render one invincible.

Vanilla Secret 1

The sun tugs fistfuls of ivy and vine stems to the cave's ceiling.
I take the Orpheus route from one world up into another
via footholds and fissures and bone dry mouths in the sheer
      rock's face
into the brightly-lit waiting room and something like wakefulness.
From the window one sees new wards under construction skeletal
scaffolds and platforms the tang of diesel fumes miserable clouds
chainsaws buzzing in the distance and she wakes to car after car
bringing women and fatherly men who will turn into fathers.

Vanilla Ghost House

The nurses' watch fobs hang upside down so we sleep all day
    like bats
weep all night in the private room while the steady drip
    of morphine
renders us half there and half not. The ghostly nurses
    roam around
in an old house stoking the fire dusting the furniture creaking
along the halls and calling out to those whose absence keeps
    them there
in white nightdresses their oil lamps held up to their
    glowing faces.
Moonlight seeps through the window as quick and silver
    as mercury
to tell us one hand is too hot and the other clean as a knife.

Vanilla Dome 3

A suit of salamander skin and gloves of stitched and
    softened tongues
and tail-lined slippers tough and fair to wear across the
    streams of fire.
His raft become automated poor Charon dosses on the banks
a penny here a penny there I would give him for his troubles.
And Dante has under it all a kingdom of ice their breaths clear
in the air down the ragged fur they climb up into the morning.

Vanilla Dome 4

A few stars are still vibrating and through the fields behind
        our house
the fox hunt tramps in uniform khaki drab fatigues desert boots.
They march as far as Solitude Bridge where the quarry
        blackly looms
and enter the woods with blunt-nosed and agitated scouting dogs
with their small calibre rifles high-powered dazzling floodlights.
I know the narrow path they take the little lake with fewer swans
year after year and fewer trout past the marshes and bulrushes.
It's the narrow path between sleep and wakefulness any minute
a gunshot the roar of a swan a stillness deeper than before.

Vanilla Secret 2

I think of the Alps edelweiss the ibex wildly scaling crags
and cliff edges but most of all I think of Ötzi the Iceman
lying in wait these few thousand years with hop-hornbeam
              in his gut
flax and poppy and sloe berries reaching out of the frozen earth
extending a frail hand as if to say I'm here it was lonely
I have longed for how it feels to be seen by someone else's eye.

Vanilla Secret 3

Arion crossing the Strait of Messina set upon by thieves
maniacal for blood and gold offered them a final music
to choose the terms of one's own death is handsomer than
     golden rings
he might have sung towards the prow and recognising destiny
between two waves stepped overboard not to drown but
     be delivered
onto dry land by a dolphin enchanted by this final song
since he was the finest player of the cithara of his day.

Vanilla Fortress

I'm swimming with the coelacanths rotting in the flooded fortress.
The unbeautiful things propel themselves in flat trajectories.
So many years we have missed you little fish little Lazarus
fossil-king of the underbite not that you knew you were missing.
They will not see me swimming here: the darkest fathoms of
     the keep
where spikes are falling from the roof and bone-machines
     roam dismally
among spine-topped anemones marauding on the castle floor.
To suffer suffer everywhere and not a moment stop to think
let the world go on without me the next life will find me happy
and adrift pedaling the swans some bright day the sun names
     the boats
one by one in the marina this will have been so long ago
by then and I will have missed you for so long will I have
     missed you.

Lemmy's Castle

In blue scrubs the Merlins apply various elixirs potions
panaceas to her body some hemostatic medicines
and a soupçon of opiate. The hospital's huge boiler plant
rumbles hums like a volcano the wards sweltering greenhouses
where all the patients start to look the same they are gradually
replaced cell by corrupted cell. At bedsides of parents children
hold it together their children play games on their little handhelds
young faces lit up in the light oblivious to the passing
moments since there is the question now of Lemmy in his castle
hiding among the heating vents confusing us with his body
doubles we would know anywhere that smile or pool of lava or
protruding from the row of pipes those legs like Breughel's Icarus.

Twin Bridges

Cheese Bridge Area

Why does it have to be like that? Why does what have to be
     like that?
Cracker Barrel. It's a weird shape. Well I don't mind. Does
     it matter?
No other cheeses are that shape. Some other cheeses are
     that shape.
It's not that really. It's just square. Well it doesn't taste square.
     It's cheese.
Maybe it's the square/cracker thing. Well not every cracker
     is square.
The crackers in the cupboard are. There are other kinds
     of crackers.
Maybe it's the Barrel part then. Well what's the problem
     with barrels?
I dream of someone throwing them. Do you know someone
     who does that?
It seems like a long time ago. It has nothing to do with cheese?
No the cheese just reminded me. Cheese can mean almost
     anything.

Cookie Mountain

Now that the cancer's been excised the clouds are
        almost meaningless
a sparrow's not a metaphor for shipping out on rocky seas
there is no creaking in the house. So I crush biscuits in a bag
add sugar and golden syrup raisins heave the mess in a tray.
Since she can't stand for very long I make tiffins for the bake sale.
No one is going to like this I say but I have done my best.
She prints her name unsteadily on a white adhesive label
for the biscuit tin that had been her mother's before it was hers
her mother's before it was hers: snow-topped mountains
        circling birds.

Soda Lake

The little rill of our river runs a mile or so to the lake
that we some Sundays would walk to. Sometimes fly-fishers on
      the banks
catching nothing drinking cider but flinging their damsel
      lures out
again and again and further. Sometimes no one but us feeding
heels of loaves to the ducks coursing in a chevron on the water
which is mostly murk and algae. Some nights it is not uncommon
to hear a salvo of gunshots bounce all along the river's length
the way a cat brings home the gift of a bird bloodied still alive.

Butter Bridge 1

Yes something to do with balance. One foot in front of the other
over the hump of the stone bridge the water slowly dismantles.
A transformer hums near it now where a scots pine
      shrugs overhead.
It's something to do with balance or it's nothing to do with it.
The way pylons repeat themselves across the fields of Herefords
the young among them gamboling then the whole herd stopped
      and staring
all those pairs of eyes bewildered the way pylons repeat themselves
a crooked line of ancestry a chain of association:
the flowers of apple blossom and apples cored in the kitchen
the pips like painted fingernails the boy kept black until the end
slowly unwoven by cancer on the inside at least he kept
the body he could see stylish at sixteen that is important.

Butter Bridge 2

The traffic on the Albert Bridge crawls stubbornly from the city.
Crews are coxed along the river by a voice through a megaphone.
This is I suppose what faith is a voice that steers into the dark.
A murmuration of starlings is a smudge on the setting sun
or the huge and happy thumbprint of Shigeru Miyamoto.

#4 Ludwig's Castle

This is the dream: it is of stone corridors of carnelian
and jasper infinite for all I know and spiked maces swinging
in the rusty reddish half-light the still air of an ossuary.
There is music too concerti and sonatas overtures suites
the acoustical buzz of skulls their jawbones almost sing along
and I almost hear the voices of the dead crow gloomy mordents
a jumble of hemiolas then the wail of an elephant
in the despair of C minor and there's him at the piano
banging away at the keyboard and spooking out the symphony
which more resembles the Virgin and Child carved out of ivory.

Forest of Illusion

Forest of Illusion 1

Whatever language the trees speak in the temple of the forest:
the knot of dark eyes signaling in the goat willow's eastern skin
or the spiny caterpillar making letters on the branches
it is familiar to me as sunset must be to nightfall.
Not to be read but understood says the trickle of the river
and without saying anything on the tree lands the butterfly
some call the Camberwell Beauty and others call the
      Mourning Cloak.

Forest of Illusion 2

Catkins drop into the river their spines gone limp they float along
its course and wind up in the lake where the rainbow trout
      spawns in spring.
I caught one once with an old rod of fibreglass and a fat worm
almost split in half on a hook and wriggling for all it was worth.
Under the dark surface flashes of colour the hook speeding off
like a silver key on the line until I stopped it with a flick
of the wrist and hoisted the fish from one world and into the next.

Blue Switch Palace

Colours sounds perfumes correspond hedgehogs wander the
      woods at night
as loud as newborn children's hair or singing like the fallow fields.
Some bird is cawing amphibrachs the colour of the gibbous moon
a mouse is coinage in the yard like motor oil or six bright stones.
Like six bright stones are sweet as milk the owl can see for
      sixteen reds
an insect moving through the grass and swoop down like a
      broken chord
and sleep then like a bag of bulbs while hedgehogs slowly start
      to rain.

Forest Ghost House

Nature is a temple of trees oboes pass the time in boxwood
I go along the narrow path so faint it's hardly even there
until the wilderness gives way to a paddock that's part
     barbed wire
part palisade where the only sound is of the passing river.
Trotting through the fenced-off clearing shoeless and a barrel
     of ribs
emaciated rheumy of eye fearful of its own body
the turmoil of its aching flanks and rickety legs a white horse.

Forest of Illusion 4

She plants roses in the garden now that the wound is
    almost healed.
With a little trowel I dig and bury the bulbs she scatters.
It's like another life she thinks the days go by in gratefulness
with amber incense gooseberries growing on gooseberry bushes.
She will not be the same of course but nor will anybody else.
Now that the wound is almost healed the nights go by so silently
that if you tried you'd almost hear the roses sleeping in their bulbs.

Forest Secret Area

High above the forest one sees the curve of the peninsula.
A farmer continues to plough whose workhorse walks dully along.
A shepherd looks out for the wolves that skulk through crags
      and crevices.
An angler seeks out plump brook trout. A Spanish galleon lingers
hugely in the bay the white sails burly with wind the conifer
mast holding snedded of branches and needles on the forest floor
the rigging like a piece of gauze in sweet and favourable winds.

Forest of Illusion 3

It's almost the end of summer and Saturday the radio
in the kitchen is a havoc of Omagh way beyond the lough
and of Slevins the chemists' shop of children running in the road
of a group of a Spanish tourists of the Assumption of Mary
insofar as it can be seen. I pause in the darkened forest.
With a dram of soap and water my brother blows bubbles all day
each of iridescent shimmer each a shallow breath in transit.

Forest Fortress

We go together to the church on the hill over the village
the wild country green behind it. In other places it's not noon
but here it is the coffin rests with a wealthiness of flowers.
My mother was a child with her. How quickly fifty years can go.
I am the light of the world says the sermon the stained
      glass window
says St Peter with rays of light. The first colour television
she ever saw was in her house my mother says and we all stand.

#5 Roy's Castle

The house's windows are undressed and with her
      old-fashioned Singer
she's putting stitches in some bolts of blue fabric the small piston
fires all through the evening and its industry of needles
runs a track through the radio softly playing Roy Orbison.
The whole world could be this one room she'll in a future
      return to
the curtains she's making all drawn against the light against July
the sewing machine ticks so fast these small years go by
      in minutes.

Chocolate Island

Chocolate Island 1

The rhinoceroses dodder like a basso ostinato
in the valleys between mountains in their scooped-out
      eroded cirques.
If there is magic in their horns they seem indifferent to it
trudging along instead upon the khaki-coloured mountain path.
I want to call them dinosaurs but that's not even kind of close:
those hundreds of millions of years that supercontinental break.
In Queensland there was that fossil showing a dinosaur stampede:
hundreds of sharp little talons but no sign of what had
      spooked them.
Thousands and thousands and thousands and thousands of
      lifetimes ago
these glyphs are all they've left behind. One clear night not so
      long ago
we all stood out in the garden wondering up at the comet
whose memory is very long who we hope still remembers us.

Choco-Ghost House

And now there's this pain in my side like a bird in the holly tree
like there was something on fire. Look how the rainclouds
    have lifted
like a bird in the holly tree there one moment and gone the next.
Look how the rainclouds have lifted. I'm thinking of a storm
    in Spain
there one moment and gone the next. I can't forget the
    lightning though.
I'm thinking of a storm in Spain and us on the wet balcony.
I can't forget the lightning though forks flashing again and again
and us on the wet balcony playing card games with the damp deck
forks flashing again and again. The huge trees came down
    around us
playing card games with the damp deck. Power lines toppled like
    ships' masts.
The tourists all ran in the streets like there was something on fire.
Power lines toppled like ships' masts and now there's this pain in
    my side.

Chocolate Island 2

As Dürer sees it under the hides of carburised iron thick
as armour plating fixed in place with rivets pinned along
      the seams
a polished gorget at the throat the rhino is mostly passive.
What he got wrong hardly matters since he'd never seen
      one himself
having just a poem a sketch imagination to go on
making magic of the mundane. And so the sun sets in the west
which is to be expected there over the marshes and deltas
I should like to describe to you having never seen them myself.

Chocolate Island 3

Sallie Gardner at a Gallop shows the horse with all four
        hooves off
the racetrack at Palo Alto California only in
frames 2 and 3 of 24. But I have known this all along
she might have told us if she could on this day half the way
        through June.
This was the year the Wright brothers saw a little helicopter
made of bamboo cork and paper with coiled rubber for a rotor
and started drawing up blueprints to leave the earth altogether.

Chocolate Secret

The precipice overlooks the valley mystic with shadow where
I glimpse again the other world a creature pacing back and forth
in a keep illuminated by the flickering of neon.
That the world unmercifully will not end is the hardest thing
that the world will go on without you and on beyond a black day
of terrific rain umbrellas snapping billowing overcoats
a day which somehow has in it the day she drove home with
     this box
seat-belted in the backseat this world the apparatus of love.

Chocolate Fortress

On a beautiful day in June we take the pain to hospital.
In through the automatic doors along the dull linoleum
past chaplaincies and children's art the infirm and the elderly.
Somewhere in the sky hangs Saturn planet of melancholia
malefic of black bile and drear. With his stethoscope slung around
his broad shoulders like an athlete with a towel Hippocrates
says for now the pain must stay here in the small room
    without flowers.
A bell does not begin to toll a goat does not begin to bleat.
In the forbidden pharmacy he goes about the magic task
of grinding down a rhino's horn to infuse with ground
    down rubies.

Chocolate Island 4

Fossicking in the mines again for citrine amethyst rose quartz
over the pools of sleech and sludge at this the nadir of the earth.
I walk the gravelly hillocks like one who walks a pilgrimage
down the long slide to crappiness it is supposed to be painful.
The spiked rocks of the cave floor sit like rotten teeth in
     rotten jaws
I walk on the rocky tongue of the planet in its open mouth
under the sad wild fearful eyes of Saturn devouring his son.

Chocolate Island 5

The sprites move in cells no taller or wider than their own bodies.
Many-faced mountains are jagged and complex as lumps
        of bismuth
the ashen land looks fire-struck and dry as the Atacama
with its mirages shimmering so convincingly I could pike
into puddles of water fronds of eelgrass swaying and come up
for air years ago in the pool of the La Mon Hotel into
its thirst and sting of chlorine and its something about to happen.

#6 Wendy's Castle

The afternoon is bright and clear as a bell tolling on the hour.
Music seeps from a radio playing at the nurses' station:
some Wendy sings her final songs in a voice low as a whisper
as bright as a shower of sparks sheared off in a welder's workshop.
Patients shuffle by with their bones emerging from their
      thinning skins
from the necklines of their kirtles their blue cotton
      hospital gowns.
So we wait in the private room turn the egg timer of ourselves.
Hippocrates in his white coat brings with him a shake of the head
brings with him the word for sorry which is the word for we
      have done
everything within our powers we have shaken out our potions
we have cast our shining magic and where we cannot do
      some good
at least we must refrain from harm. And the traffic lights
      are changing
and the traffic will dribble on along the busy carriageway
towards the beach or barbecues because it's the summer solstice.
And then the talk of opiates of comfort and what's possible
of a cloak threaded with morphine another castle to die in.
I'm sorry she wanted to say my body won't cooperate
my body's become overcome though she did not say anything
but stared as if to recall how my face looked when she first saw me.

Valley of Bowser

Sunken Ghost Ship

Not a warship but a merchant brigantine adrift disheveled
but seaworthy with no crewman or passenger footing its decks
having set off for Genoa from New York many years ago.
The story goes the ship was found abandoned in beautiful trim
with every sail set not a rope out of place fire in the grate
400 miles from the Azores. The passengers weren't seen again.
Deep blue sea I ask no questions of you deep blue sea tell no lies.
Still here swells a sense of falling down through the bottom of
     the world.
One takes a last breath of this world and closes one's eyes
     and descends.

Valley of Bowser 1

Like a labyrinth of neural pathways one encounters dead ends
and blind alleys and cul de sacs all of which are really the same
save to say there are various ways of finding oneself lost there:
lost like rain on the Atlantic lost in the garden I planted
my name I wrote on old cardboard I remember now the shepherds'
red sky and all through to morning the secateurs snapping thickly
and when a woman came to cut our hair she seldom remembered
our names mistaking my brother for me for a pair of scissors.

Valley of Bowser 2

On through the valley of shadow shifting strata mazes of dirt
walls closing like mine collapses or morphine's tightness in
      the chest
its heaviness and its terror. A fountain drips in the courtyard
birds do motets and madrigals although the birds are seldom seen.
Some things we choose to disregard: the cruelty of newspapers
the casual chat of holidays the world and how it now appears.
Henry comes up how young and fine and dead now nearly
      fifty years.
How the telegram sent received said only YOUR SON
      HENRY DEAD.
How expensive to correspond all that way from Tasmania.
This is how the visitors talk without saying what they're thinking.
After not so long she's dozed off. The ancient voice of her brother
who wanders through the corridors takes on the clean sound
      of scissors
or the sound of water leaking from the mouth of a broken tap.

Valley Fortress

These are the days of no letters her signature starved with jitters
in the few half hours she's awake to make arrangements:
     no flowers
or no more than is natural for a swift discreet funeral
and burial with her parents tea and sandwiches afterwards.
She sleeps the undertaker leaves the fountain leaks in
     the courtyard.
My head is heavier than stone. I read yesterday's newspapers
eat crisps from the vending machine I want to die is what she says
not either asleep or awake let me please die is what she says.
It's me I'm here is what I say but I am not since she is not.
Then she says I want to go home once more for one once more
     one night
and I say you can't go home now she says I know not now after.

Valley Ghost House

Bright brother it is you I seek in the cobwebs in the alcoves
as though images of us still roam there or are in the future.
Anyway should you some evening hear that creak or keen
    of timber
on the landing think of the house we grew up in the begonias
patterned across the stairs the fuzz of the carpet against
    your cheek
think that this creaking now is just us long ago when we
    were young:
the toy trains zooming through the rooms the secret door in
    the hedgerows
where hosts of robins passing make exactly the sound of the wind.

Valley of Bowser 3

It's so short she says it's so short it doesn't feel like I've been here
at all and now I have to go. The bluish light is from a lamp.
The portable television we brought from home is standing by.
I won't get to see what happens to you or your brother she says
as if our lives were determined already along one sure path.
No grandchildren and no first steps and never again a first word.
My first word she says was apple or something something
    like apple.

Valley of Bowser 4

So it's one who wears a cuirass who spends the evening
      throwing stones
from the vantage-points afforded by his high and
      wretched prospect.
Where is the one who planted vines that beanstalk out of
      their boxes?
Where is kindness its parishes its empty hand its open arms?
Over swells of lava over severe drops and quarter circles
swept out of the rock I'm compelled to witness the long
      days shorten.
Is it so that every world is only a world of enemies?
I've been here so long I think I hear my children passing the door.
Should I go to the door though there is only night and its garden
suddenly not my dream but hers and she dreams of us arriving.

#7 Larry's Castle

Elsewhere I slept as the rattle started like an engine that cranks
moans and whinnies but never starts or a wound clock whose
    key is lost.
No clock ticks in her room but if one speaks light fluently one can
tell the time by the shadow the fountain casts across
    the courtyard.
Hippocrates arrives again and I ask him what will happen.
Today is the day yes I guess and what am I to say to her
asleep he says but still aware a voice speaking a floor below
my voice warped into the scribble of a child in soot or lampblack
what kind of story do I tell apple is the longest story
I know let's see how does it go again apple apple apple.

PART TWO

Star World

Star World 1

I dug with the heels of my boots ingloriously gradual.
One afternoon we transplanted a rose bush that blossomed yearly
in memory of her mother to the middle of the garden
so she'd see it from the window if she raised her head to look out.
I dug against the bony earth the holly tree's nebulous roots
throughout the garden I slackened more than once her final winter
though we didn't know it yet the robins nesting in the branches
would be gone by summer when she returns to the room she
     looked from
lit up once by joy and light the room above which I cannot sleep.

Star World 2

A deep breath I am water tight on the ocean floor an egg cracks.
I proceed invincibly I dream alone and dauntless into
the realms of blue-headed wrasses sleeping the sleep of the fishes
dreaming with the rhizomatic samphire (*dreadful trade*) they
       once called
glasswort since with the opposite of water fire artisans
transform its ashes into glass on which Saint Peter smiles a smile
of light stopped on the window and speaks the opposite of water.

Star Road 3

I walk into the night as it aches all over the countryside
tramping under the ruptured path of the milky way the moon-blue
swoop of the road pointed homeward say goodnight
      volcanic columns
so long rolling glens and valleys. The streetlights fur
      like hyacinths
like beacons and their intervals mentioning across the landscape
that war has come that villages are sacked that men lie in the mud
fortifications in ruins the howls of widows and orphans
like nettles the stinging of smoke and hours later when I awake
in my childhood bed there's embers dozing in the warm fireplace.

Star Road 4

The troika platforms turbine through another boiling night
  of stars
of the distances between them of chaos which is nothingness
through the valley rolls a chaos. In the chaos of the night sky
I would find a key and keyhole a way out yes but into what
the strange passing from one blue world into another world
  of blue
most mysterious frequency since for so long no one could speak
of it and since when blue could be mentioned the old world
   was ended
by a new colour of all things by indigo or common woad
by blue this most expensive shade the calm blue of hospice carpets
this blue by its presence welcomes the ritual of the new world.

Star Road 5

The Colorado river ran and ran to shape the Grand Canyon
and now it is filled up with night right to the brim and
      more beyond
night spills up to whatever is not night pulsars pulse I traverse
the chasm which is both nothing and rock around it sending back
the second guess of an echo which of the voices is my voice
how sarcasm offers two thoughts at once one inside the other.
My friends are scattered on ranges along the island's
      wave-wrecked coast
and turtle doves skidoo above mesas and yellow columbines.
She spends a final night at home. I have gone to rescue my friends.

Special World

Gnarly

I tried to make a monument out of the pink wisteria
and to shape from the lands of light cartilage from cartography
from rolling green and glowing plains and five-jointed
      springboard launchers
and vines that beanstalk from a box cumulus cumulonimbus
cirrus attended by sun dogs seen by ships at sea soon to sink
from forests of pupae furies of carnelian or ruby
from countless spiny crawling sprites duplicated as pathogens
from Osterberg and Orbison and Beethoven and Nine Inch Nails
from anthropomorphic stone heads in fortresses near far and wide
from falling dreams sweet streams that flow the length of the
      garden planted
with roses and honeysuckle with foxgloves and wild funguses
I tried to make a monument from the cathode rays
      blasting streams
of electrons behind a screen from quarries foxhunts and gunshots
from ghillies dipped low in Flecktarn scouting the forest on
      the hill
I want my monument to be composed of light as you might say
so you can see it friend not things themselves but the seeing
      of them
the light stopping on them tree I adore you I adore you world.

Tubular

The roughed-off ends of pipes comprise a windless skyline citadel
as though they're waiting for music if someone had the breath
     for it
and anyway doesn't the wind distribute breath around the world
the wind never again striking her shoulders for those final breaths
I wasn't there we had driven to McDonald's of all places
the sun low on the carriageway *Diamonds on the Soles of her Shoes*
on the radio the rasp of the handbrake the gravelled courtyard
the blue carpets of the hallways. With whatever strength she
     had left
she went without me as witness devotion I can't imagine.
I will myself to contain it: a paean labouring under
so many feet I have taken in a breath of the world so huge
the rest of my life will be spent breathing the world into the world.

Way Cool

I tried to make a monument from the Television's On/Off
button whose once-black surface has been worn away to silver by
thousands of thumbs over the years and its hiss and buzz of static
a monument of its glass screen dense as bone or maybe the moon
or the shock of aspidistra in a pot of terracotta
on a mock Queen Anne side table or a needlework from Henry's
widow in Queensland in silver and gold depicting two dancers
dancing in the style of John Luke O never never canst thou kiss.
The clock tick tocks at a gallop in the tiled cavern of the hall
sunset is drawn to the part-stained part-frosted glass of the
        front door.
Every other day I think I see her passing by the window
or crossing a bridge or walking ahead of me in the village
but this is the wrong universe among all the universes.

Awesome

A morning all of wintergreen the snow has closed the
    country roads
our house is white among the white fields the forest white on
    the hill
the river ripples freezing sines all the way to Solitude Bridge
to the main stream spume and spindrift the waters of the
    Irish Sea.
I walk for no reason along the middle of the purple road:
no traffic no people for miles and for no reason except for
being alone I try to scream into the wildness of the world.
I make no sound: the flakes of snow are noisier in their falling
the berries are loud with colour on the back windowsill a bird
has written its name in footprints a handful of steps at the door.
The voice is made of whatever is left how the world is dented.
Dear friends I cannot rescue you anymore than I can place her
shoulders in the way of the wind but when you're walking in
    the snow
when the time comes there's room for you in this voice because
    it's your voice.

Groovy

I tried to make a monument from the emptiness of the house:
the house in which everything starts the berries and
      scarps cactuses
inching along in the verdure mosses clinging to water pipes
but nothing would explain itself and things would
      only correspond.
The house empty but for me is a highway in the wilderness
is a river in the desert is a blue eye in the kettle
is a candle made of water is a photograph on fire
is a church bell in the graveyard is a letter I can't open
is a forest at Chernobyl is a beached whale at Donegal
is fair lined slippers for the cold is buckles of the purest gold
is the fox hunt stalking the fields is the fox guarding the henhouse
is the cat among the pigeons is the creak up in the rafters
when I returned to the empty house it was no longer empty.

Mondo

The waves the waves undulating the waves undulating flotsams
the waves undulating flotsams of belly-up fishes drowning
the poem breathes underwater in the canals of Venice long
before I am born before she is married the gondolas cut
the glinting water the sun huge as she (young) orbits it the sound
of our river trickles up to the bridge and she can hear now these
sun-tempered waters of Venice fountains in the hospice courtyard
two Saturns of memory big jumble sale of the mind morphine
how much does this thing cost (darling) whatever do you call
      this thing?
In this her box of bric-à-brac a photo of a gondolier
a charm of blue Murano glass flashes of copper and cobalt
explaining themselves to the light. In the quietness of the house
the hush of the river running its capillary is sounded
in a voice like someone else's running away under the hills
where we can't follow communing with other waters emerging
as a torrent that spills into the lake now it's my voice she hears.

Outrageous

So suddenly was the summer over like a bellows days shrank
the fireplace puffed out embers that flickered and
      soon extinguished
where over the hearth soot began to sign its name firewood sat
in a pile of splinters the tree tallest in the forest lightning
felled I went there to the forest up on the hill behind our house
I frolicked and tramped through the mud to a place I thought no
      one else
had ever been before it was so deep into the wilderness
finding instead in a clearing hunters' leavings: cold fire pits
rusting tin cans the casings of distinct calibres of weapon
a fox hunt discarded passing through the fields like a noisy moon
the sparks of munitions lighting up their faces I imagine
some quarry in his den of earth the pillars of trees labyrinthine
witnesses: speak aloud these words the tall tree of the ear I put
my head against the fireplace that with a deep breath the embers
might confess to me what they've seen while the room fills up
      with their warmth.

Funky

The little sumo thunder gods shiko little bolts of lightning
the sky storm-dark as it has been these blue afternoons of winter
the garden is overgrowing a gooseberry splits on my tongue
full of the thinking of robins full of the odour of ozone.
I travelled back to other storms semibreves of rolling thunder
waiting finally for the flash a gooseberry splits on my tongue
and sixteen years have disappeared thousands of berries in
		the trees
like Christmases robins hop by their breasts a swell of
		ground rubies
while the roses swell and recede the begonias swell and recede
homeless Saturn is halfway home the beautiful television
decomposes in a landfill the hard ground softens the soft ground
softens the hard ground the holly roots bristle
		suspended throughout
in the garden I buried my name I wanted it to be found.
Should I pray to gods of thunder or the wounded gods of myself
the storm crumbles the bank into the river and what can I say
this has not been easy thank you friend you are a super reader.

* * *

Front Door

In through the translucent panels of the front door stained
     with roses
here and there their green stems wander sun patterns the
     cavernous hall
with rose outlines the wood paneled box came sharp-cornered
     the TV
so heavy to look at it cut into my clavicle was it
full of cannonballs and was it carried on four or six or eight
sets of shoulders into the room such impossible heaviness
for the size of it and was it full of tinctures puzzled colours
picture elements their sweep rates flashing across it when I saw
my reflection in the blackness of its face it was a child's face.
Neighbours came over their fences a summer day but dark
     with storms:
a deluge impassible roads the forest lurching on the hill.
I felt my head turn into stone no it wasn't the old TV
we carried her to the window the meteors that time of year
Perseids only sparks really the Irish Sea fell from the sky
in bullets through the afternoon and Kong Kappa no King Koopa
navigates his ship through the storm an engine or
     thunder rumbles.
Electrons pooled under the clouds the room was heavy with ions.
I held my breath in the lightning the sea fell into the garden.
Evening rose like the river then the flash with all of us in it
and her voice moves around the edge of the world and now I
     think I
remember what I mean to say which is only to say that once
when all the world and love was young I saw it beautiful glowing
once in the corner of the room once I was sitting in its light.

The End

CREDITS

(In order of appearance)

My house, Yoshi, hallucinogenic mushrooms (*Amanita muscaria*), mitosis, my mother, photography, light, the Lotus Position, economy, Kappa (Japanese mythological creature), television, Holly (*Ilex aquifolium*), Robins (*Erithacus rubecula*), Ivy (Hedera), Blackthorn (Prunus spinosa), Groundsel (*Senecio vulgaris*), Daisy (*Bellis perennis*), Petrarch (1304–1374), 'Ascent of Mount Ventoux', my brother, Genoa, my father, turtle dove (*Streptopelia turtur*), things with spines, Saguaro cactus (*Carnegiea gigantean*), Bangor, swan pedalo, Chemotheraphy, insomnia, Iggy and the Stooges, the Scoville Scale, Northern Ireland, Delftware, Lough Neagh, Sargasso Sea, eels, Syacmore (*Acer pseudoplatanus*), family photographs, Henry Smyth (d. 1964), Assisted Passage Migration Scheme, mining, mine collapse, Jacques Derrida, emeralds, Iron pyrite, stone cottages, Andrew Marvell (1621–1678), 'The Garden', Michael Donaghy (1954–2004), 'Haunts', Pigeon (*Columba palumbus*), Sparrow (*Passer domesticus*), William Shakespeare (1564–1616), *The Tempest*, Shepherds (singing), Wrasse (*Thalassoma bifasciatum*), Tilapia (*Oreochromis niloticus*), Hogfish (*Lachnolaimus maximus*), Dogfish (*Squalus acanthias*), Catfish (*Silurus glanis*), Salmon (*Salmo salar*), Tuna (*Thunnus thynnus*), Sunfish (*Mola mola*), Anglerfish (*Melanocetus johnsonii*), the Mariana Trench, Ulster Hospital, McDonald's, Nintendo Game Boy, Sagittarius, Carrick-a-Rede Rope Bridge, chestnuts, the First World War (1914–1918), acetone, cordite, Fairy Rings, a Surgeon, Surgery,

Anaesthesia, Johnny Cash (1932–2003), 'Dark as a Dungeon', Kimberly Diamond mine, South Africa, time, the Big Hole, rowboats, spelunking, Sharaska, alchemy, alternative therapies, climbing, Orpehus, childbirth, nurses' watch fobs, bats (*Pipistrellus pipistrellus*), Morphine, moonlight, Mercury, Salamander (*Salamandra salamandra*), Charon, Dante Aligheri (1265–1321), *The Divine Comedy*, vantage points, fox-hunting, Solitude Bridge, swans (*Cygnus olor*), trout (*Oncorhynchus mykiss*), bulrushes (*Typha latifolia*), gunfire, the Alps, edelweiss (*Leontopodium alpinum*), Ötzi the Iceman (d. c. 3500 BC), hop-hornbeam (*Ostrya carpinifolia*), flax (*Linum usitatissimum*), poppy (*Papaver somniferum*), Arion of Messina, dolphins, cithara, Coelocanth (*Latimeria chalumnae*), Lazarus of Bethany, Anemone (*Epiactis prolifera*), The Hospital, wizards, medical professionals, hemostatic medicines, opiates, video games, doppelgängers, Motorhead, Lemmy Kilminster (1945–2015), Pieter Bruegel (1525–1569), 'Landscape with the Fall of Icarus', Virgil's Eclogues, Cracker Barrel (cheese), Ducks (*Anas platyrhynchos*), Cat (*Felis catus,*) Donkey Kong, Cancer, Clouds, Baking, a biscuit tin, a river, the lake, Sunday, Fly-Fishing, Damselflies (*Ischnura heterosticta*), a walk to the lake, Scots Pine (*Pinus sylvestris L.*), Pylons, Herefords, Apple Blossom (*Malus domestica*), Goths, death, fashion, The Albert Bridge, rowers on the river Lagan, Starling (*Sturnus vulgaris*), Shigeru Miyamoto (1952–), Ludwig van Beethoven (1770–1827), 'Fifth Symphony', Jasper, Carnelian, an ossuary, trills, piano, E Flat Major, Virgin and Child, Forests, Charles Baudelaire (1821–1867), 'Correspondances', Goat willow (Salix caprea), Caterpillar (*Agonopterix pallorella*), Camberwell Beauty (*Nymphalis antiopa*), Fishing, cruelty, underwater, the elements, synesthesia, Hedgehog (*Erinaceus europaeus*), metrical feet, Wood Mouse (Apodemus sylvaticus), Oboes, a clearing in the woods, first born children, mistreatment of animals, a white horse (*Equus ferus caballus*), convalescence, planting roses in the garden, amber, incense, gooseberries (*Ribes uva-crispa*), Ekphrasis, brook trout, (*Salvelinus fontinalis*), a Spanish Galleon, explosives, The Omagh Bomb (15th August 1998), the Assumption of

Mary, a funeral, half a century, St Peter (d. 64), stained glass, colour television, a Singer sewing machine, the radio, Roy Orbison (1936–1988), making curtains, Rhinoceros (*Rhinoceros unicornis*), basso ostinato, mountainous areas, the breakup of Pangaea, Dinosaurs, palaeontology, Queensland, fossils, texts, Hale-Bopp, Storms in Spain, card games (Jack Change It), armour-plating, Albrecht Dürer (1471–1528), *Rhinoceros*, the imagination, recalcitrance, Eadweard Muybridge (1830–1904), *Sallie Gardner at a Gallop*, California, The Wright Brothers, Alphonse Pénaud (1850–1880), death, funeral, Super Nintendo Entertainment System, June, hospital, abdominal pain, Saturn Return, Hippocrates (*c.* 460–*c.* 370 B.C.), Albrecht Dürer (1471–1528), *Melencolia I*, angiogenisis inhibitors, Philip Larkin (1922–1985), 'High Windows', precious stones, Francisco Goya (1746–1828), *Saturn Devouring His Son*, reverberation, cell destruction, bismuth, the Atacama Desert, eelgrass (*Zostera marina*), The La Mon Hotel, silence, kirtles, skeletons, sparks, sorry, palliative care, a hospice, Wendy O Williams (1949–1998), Marie Celeste, New York, Ghost Ships, shipwreck, the Azores, mysteries, Philip Larkin (1922–1985), 'The Whitsun Weddings', Memory, the Atlantic Ocean, becoming lost, secateurs, haircuts, mistaken identity, scissors, valleys, strata, mazes, dirt, visitors to the dying, a dripping fountain, choral music performed by birds, a telegram, letters, signature, funeral preparations, an old house, toy trains, ghosts, the shortness of life, first steps, first words, armour, stone-throwing, dismay, enmity, eternity, a future, a dream of us arriving, a failing engine, apples, Louis MacNeice (1907–1963), 'Snow', rosebushes, robins, winter, in memoriam, grandmothers, digging, horticulture, fatigue, migration, wake, swimming, rebirth, sea creatures, sleeping with the fishes, artisans, William Shakespeare (1564–1616), *King Lear*, glasswort (*Crithmum maritimum*), stained glass, Pentecost, elemental forces, Vincent Van Gogh (1853–1890), *The Starry Night*, Anne Sexton (1928–1974), 'The Starry Night', The Giant's Causeway, Co. Antrim, volcanoes, basalt, masquerades, Fancy Dress Parties, transmigration of the soul, the milky way, the moon, Zephyrus, hyacinths, sacked villages, a dream, The Colorado River, the Grand Canyon, thresholds of worlds, the colour blue, indigo, woad, a Hospice, chaos pulsars, quasars, infinity, sarcasm, absent friends, mesas, columbines, nothing, monuments, memorials, wisteria (*Wisteria sinensis*), cartography, Jack and the Beanstalk, clouds, sun dogs (atmospheric phenomenon), sinking ships, pupae, carnelian, ruby, pathogens, James Newell Osterberg (b. 1947), Roy Orbison (1936–1988), Trent Reznor (b. 1965), falling dreams, Stranmillis, cathode rays, ghillie suits, Flecktarn, drainage pipes, plumbing, paeans, respiration, Paul Simon (1941–), 'Diamonds on the Soles of Her Shoes', the death of my mother (1952–2012), televisions, thumbs, bone, moon, aspidistra, terracotta, Queen Anne (fashion), needlework, widows, John Luke (1906–1975), John Keats (1795–1821), clocks, sunset, the wrong universe, road closures, the Irish Sea, screaming, footprints in the snow, empty houses, The Uncanny, Chernobyl, beaching (of whales), Donegal, Christopher Marlowe (1564–1593), 'The Passionate Shepherd to His Love', The Pastoral, tidal movements, Venice, breathing underwater, gondolas, Saturn (planet), gondoliers, Murano glass, William Shakespeare (1564–1616), *Othello*, lightning, felled trees, the forest behind my house, canned food, bullet casings, Rainer Maria Rilke (1875–1926), *Sonnets to Orpheus*, sumo wrestling, gooseberries, time dilation, ozone, sixteen years, Christmas, begonias, landfills, thunder gods, most excellent and generous readers (you), the front door to my house, televisions, coffins, teamwork, weight, reflections, neighbours, heavy rain, the Perseids, King Koopa, Bowser, beautiful lights.

ACKNOWLEDGEMENTS

So many thanks to Maria Bedford, Sarah Wright, Micca Wright, Tom Etherington and everyone at Penguin, and to Tracy Bohan for her incredible support and belief.

I'm grateful to Sally Rooney for publishing demo versions in *The Stinging Fly*, to Damian Smyth and the Arts Council of Northern Ireland, and to Maureen Kennelly, Paul Lenehan and Elizabeth Mohen at Poetry Ireland for their encouragement and generosity, and to Emma Wright and Rachel Piercy and The Emma Press.

Thanks to colleagues and advisors at the Seamus Heaney Centre: Leontia Flynn, Gail McConnell, Fran Brearton, Glenn Patterson, Rachel Brown, Jimmy McAleavey and Nick Laird, and to Colin Graham, Edna and Michael Longley, Paula Meehan, Theo Dorgan and Paul Maddern. Particular thanks to Sinéad Morrissey for her brilliance, and for helping me understand what I was trying to say, and to *il professore, il maestro*, Ciaran Carson, to whom I am indebted and to whom language itself is indebted.

Much gratitude to Padraig Regan for their imagination and for many conversations, to Daire Moffat, Michael Nolan, Tom Morris, Stephen Connolly, Manuela Moser, Tara McEvoy, Caitlin Newby, Dane Holt, Sacha White, Scott McKendry, Andy Eaton, Dave Coates, Darragh McCausland, Cal Doyle, Wayne Miller, and to Mary Denvir and the legend of Bookfinders Café, and of course to these boys: Nathan Lynch, James Gilpin, Michael Weir, John Culbert, Ryan Wiles.

Love to Bríd, always.

Yoshi's House

May this unhaunted house be yours and may it be happy
    and bright.
May the creak in the rafters be a sparrow returning to nest
after all these years and before the many more I step aside.
And if you find some day dear friend my sad head upon on
    your shoulders
go out into the world say world it's been so long say world hello.